The Spokesman

How to Lose a War

Edited by Ken Coates

Published by Spokesman for the
Bertrand Russell Peace Foundation

Spokesman 90   2006

CONTENTS

Editorial	3	Ken Coates
Vice Visits Virtue	6	Arundhati Roy
Nato: Expanding or Exploding?	8	Gabriel Kolko
War in Iraq: Time to Go!	11	John P Murtha
Three Poems	14	Christopher Hampton
Dispatch from a Man without a Country	16	Kurt Vonnegut
UN: Quis custodiet ipsos custodes?	28	Denis Halliday interviewed by David Barsamian
Europe and Extraordinary Rendition	35	Tony Bunyan
Drawn To That Moment	40	John Berger
Peace Dossier	46	Beyond Abu Ghraib Seeking the missing in Iraq 'Strive for nuclear disarmament' Vanunu reports
Reviews	69	Henry McCubbin Ken Coates Michael Barratt Brown Michael Foot Richard Fletcher

Printed by the Russell Press Ltd., Nottingham, UK

SN 0262 7922   ISBN 0 85124 724 5

Subscriptions

Institutions £30.00/€60/$60
Individuals £20.00 (UK)
£25.00 (ex UK)
€40/$40

Back issues available on request

A CIP catalogue record for this book is available from the British Library

Index: www.altpress.org

Published by the
Bertrand Russell Peace Foundation Ltd.,
Russell House
Bulwell Lane
Nottingham NG6 0BT
England
Tel. 0115 9784504
email:
elfeuro@compuserve.com
www.spokesmanbooks.com
www.russfound.org

Editorial Board:
Michael Barratt Brown
Ken Coates
John Daniels
Ken Fleet
Stuart Holland
Tony Simpson

Make sure you are treated with dignity at work

Join Amicus today

Join online at www.amicustheunion.org
or contact us free on 0800 587 1222

Amicus: the modern union for you

Editorial
How to Lose a War

The crisis of non-proliferation comes to a head in the present scary confrontation with Iran. The kept press in the United States, but sadly, also in Europe, monotonously informs us that the Iranians are in the various stages of preparing to manufacture an arsenal of nuclear weapons. There is no real evidence of this, although it is freely admitted by the Iranian Government that it is determined to pursue the development of nuclear power stations.

President Ahmadinejad, who is not always famous for his temperate statements, has never wavered in one commitment: that Iran has no use for nuclear bombs, and indeed that their use is not consonant with the behaviour of a genuine Muslim. Recently, there was a strong statement by President Khatami, which gently corrected his successor's view of the holocaust, speaking of it as 'a historical reality'. Khatami went on to say, 'We should speak out if even a single Jew is killed. Don't forget that one of the crimes of Hitler, Nazism and German National Socialism was the massacre of innocent people, among them many Jews.' It was, of course, possible for Hitler to massacre millions of people without having at his command the use of a single nuclear bomb. But by contrast it is not possible to use a nuclear bomb without guaranteeing the deaths of very large numbers of people who are completely innocent of any part in any conflict. Iranians are aware of this.

Circumstances alter cases. Not so long ago, Richard B. Cheney, Paul Wolfowitz, Donald Rumsfeld and President Gerald Ford used all their powerful advocacy to urge upon the Iranian Government the need to buy, from the United States, expensive reprocessing equipment and other facilities for the extraction of plutonium from nuclear reactor fuel. In August 1974, Donald Rumsfeld, soon to become Chief of Staff of the White House, and a member of the President's Cabinet (before he went on to the Secretaryship of Defence from 1975-7), was one of those who endorsed the Iranian plan to build up a substantial nuclear energy industry. He 'also worked hard to complete a multi-billion dollar deal that would have given Tehran control of large quantities of plutonium and enriched uranium – the two pathways to a nuclear bomb'.

Today, the Bush administration claims it to be an axiom of its foreign policy that, almost at any cost, it needs to prevent Iran from achieving exactly those capacities which members of the predecessor administration were encouraging Iran to acquire, thirty years earlier. Of course, the Iran in question was a trusted ally of the United States, ruled by the Shah and his iron-gripped SAVAK Secret Police. Today, the Iranian Government is a valued component of the axis of evil, which should not be allowed to develop as much as a catapult if only the American administration knew how to limit such technology.

The hysteria which greets the civil nuclear programme of Iran marks a culminating moment in the uprooting of the Non-Proliferation Treaty. That Treaty marked a voluntary commitment to renounce nuclear weapons, when an insane Cold War competition seemed to rational men and women all around the world to pose a severe threat to the survival of humanity. Purely voluntarily, nations agreed to renounce the prospect of the military use of atomic energy. Ultimately, it was agreed, existing nuclear states would follow the same path, forswearing, by mutual agreement, the nuclear arsenals of which they already disposed. This commitment peaked in the year 2000, when the NPT Review process agreed on steps to accomplish this disarmament of existing nuclear powers.

Notwithstanding the agreement, nothing whatever was done to bring it to implementation. Instead, the idea of non-proliferation was subtly replaced by an altogether more sinister concept of *counter*-proliferation. This implies action to disarm proliferators or would-be proliferators. Who will take such action? Why, of course, an existing nuclear power, who will thus be acknowledged to be a universal policeman, although no one has ever proposed it for this role, nominated it to be keeper of the nuclear covenant, or even understood that it was hungering for the task. The counter-proliferators are out in force, barking at the heels of Iran.

In a worthy response to this frenzy, numerous people have raised the question of the Israeli bomb, about which interesting revelations have been coming out of the British Foreign Office, which apparently facilitated its development. According to Mordechai Vanunu, who served many years in prison for revealing the truth about what had been happening while he worked in the Israeli plant at Dimona, the Israelis have been developing thermo-nuclear bombs, and have long held an arsenal of some two hundred 'normal' nukes. The Arab League, and numerous other witnesses, have cogently argued that the West is showing double standards, in leaving the all-too-actual Israeli bomb unchallenged, whilst energetically pursuing the phantom arsenal of Iran. This is very clearly a repetition of the celebrated dodgy dossier, which, the reader may remember, helped take Britain and the United States to war in Iraq, to destroy numerous non-existent weapons of mass destruction.

There is still work for the nuclear researchers to do, in uncovering the precise relationship between Israel and South Africa, in the development of that bomb. Since the early 1980s, there have been repeated allegations that the Israelis had been co-operating with South Africa and Taiwan. In a fog of denials, a number of possible Israeli-South African nuclear explosions were reported in the world's press. Test facilities were alleged to exist in the Kalahari Desert, and three significant explosions were detected in the South Atlantic in December 1980.

The ending of apartheid put an end to the South African bomb, or at any rate, that part of it which did not go home to Israel. But perhaps the South African connection might help to explain why some British civil servants were so keen to help to furnish the Israelis with the wherewithal to complete the only genuine act of nuclear proliferation which has yet unfolded in the Middle East.

Will all the foaming at the mouth about the Iranian bomb lead to new invasions, and new outbreaks of shock and awe? Some Americans appear to think that the Iranians can, with impunity, be punished at arm's length with bunker-busters and so prevented from pursuing the weapons which they say they have never wanted in the first place. This is a very doubtful prospect. If one thing could unite a fairly divided, if not pluralistic, public opinion in Iran, surely it would be visitations from American bombers. There is absolutely no reason why the Iranians should sit still and allow their tormentors to punish them at will.

We already have some of the predictions about the course of this unlikely war: crude oil at more than one hundred dollars a barrel; the blocking of the Straits of Hormuz, the famous 'chokepoint', which can be squeezed to disrupt worldwide oil flows; angry Iraqi Shia pursuit of allied forces. All these and more reprisals are not only feasible, but may be likely if the madcap scheme for the culminating war is not called off or stopped. Of course, sane voices in the United States are telling us all the time that the ground forces do not exist to carry through any new American offensive. Frantic efforts are made to embroil troops from Nato, but these are more likely to backfire than not. It may indeed be Nato itself which is the main victim of such schemes.

There is some evidence that the Bush design for the Middle East might be about to end. Certainly it will end in tears. But what will follow it? Is there no hopeful prospect for the world, or are we to await a succession of grandiose onslaughts, as this most extraordinary military power seeks to substitute bombs for brains. If we could give brains a chance, might it not be possible also to give peace a chance?

Ken Coates

IAEA says no evidence of Iranian nuclear weapons plan

DUBAI: As the countdown for a crucial meeting on Iran on March 6 gets under way, the International Atomic Energy Agency (IAEA) has revealed that it has not found any evidence that Tehran had diverted material towards making atomic weapons. In its report which has been circulated to its 35 board members, the IAEA said that its three years of investigations had not shown 'any diversion of nuclear material to nuclear weapons or other nuclear explosive devices', the Associated Press reported. However, it called upon Iran to substantially increase its cooperation with the IAEA inspectors as the agency has not been able 'to conclude that there are no undeclared nuclear materials or activities in Iran.'

Without heightened cooperation, the agency would be unable to establish whether some of Iran's past nuclear activities under wraps were not linked to the manufacture of nuclear weapons. Iranian Foreign Minister Manouchehr Mottaki who has been visiting Japan said, 'They (IAEA) could not find evidence which shows that Iran has diverted from its peaceful purposes of nuclear activities in Iran.'

On February 4, the board had decided to report Iran's case to the UN Security Council, which can take action against Iran, including the imposition of economic sanctions. Buoyed by the report, Iran is rushing the head of its Supreme National Security Council (SNSC) Ali Larijani to Russia for another round of talks. A Russian delegation led by Sergei Kiriyenko held talks with Iran over the weekend. These discussions had revolved around the establishment of a joint venture facility in Russia, which would produce enriched uranium for generating electricity. That meeting produced an 'agreement in principle' on this subject.

However, later, differences appear to have surfaced on another issue – on whether Iran would be allowed to operate a small-scale enrichment plant for research purposes. The IAEA report said that Iran had begun enrichment using 10 centrifuges – a move which can result in the production of only minute quantities of enriched uranium.

Atul Aneja, *The Hindu*, 1 March 2006

Vice Visits Virtue

Arundhati Roy

On his triumphalist tour of India and Pakistan, where he hopes to wave imperiously at people he considers potential subjects, President Bush has an itinerary that's getting curiouser and curiouser.

For Bush's March 2 pit stop in New Delhi, the Indian government tried very hard to have him address our parliament. A not inconsequential number of MPs threatened to heckle him, so Plan One was hastily shelved. Plan Two was to have Bush address the masses from the ramparts of the magnificent Red Fort, where the Indian prime minister traditionally delivers his Independence Day address. But the Red Fort, surrounded as it is by the predominantly Muslim population of Old Delhi, was considered a security nightmare. So now we're into Plan Three: President George Bush speaks from Purana Qila, the Old Fort.

Ironic, isn't it, that the only safe public space for a man who has recently been so enthusiastic about India's modernity should be a crumbling medieval fort?

Since the Purana Qila also houses the Delhi zoo, George Bush's audience will be a few hundred caged animals and an approved list of caged human beings, who in India go under the category of 'eminent persons.' They're mostly rich folk who live in our poor country like captive animals, incarcerated by their own wealth, locked and barred in their gilded cages, protecting themselves from the threat of the vulgar and unruly multitudes whom they have systematically dispossessed over the centuries.

So what's going to happen to George W. Bush? Will the gorillas cheer him on? Will the gibbons curl their lips? Will the brow-antlered deer sneer? Will the chimps make rude noises? Will the owls hoot? Will the lions yawn and the giraffes bat their beautiful eyelashes? Will the crocs recognize a kindred soul? Will the quails give thanks that Bush isn't travelling with Dick Cheney, his hunting partner with the notoriously bad aim? Will the CEOs agree?

Arundhati Roy's books include An Ordinary Person's Guide To Empire, Public Power in the Age of Empire *and the prize-winning novel* The God of Small Things.

Oh, and on March 2, Bush will be taken to visit Gandhi's memorial in Rajghat. He's by no means the only war criminal who has been invited by the Indian government to lay flowers at Rajghat. (Only recently we had the Burmese dictator General Than Shwe, no shrinking violet himself.) But when Bush places flowers on that famous slab of highly polished stone, millions of Indians will wince. It will be as though he has poured a pint of blood on the memory of Gandhi.

We really would prefer that he didn't.

It is not in our power to stop Bush's visit. It is in our power to protest it, and we will. The government, the police and the corporate press will do everything they can to minimize the extent of our outrage. Nothing the happy newspapers say can change the fact that all over India, from the biggest cities to the smallest villages, in public places and private homes, George W. Bush, the President of the United States of America, world nightmare incarnate, is just not welcome.

RMT

For **Peace** and **International Solidarity**

Bob Crow
General Secretary

Tony Donaghey
President

Nato: Expanding or Exploding?

Gabriel Kolko

Gabriel Kolko is the foremost historian of warfare. His latest book, The Age of War: The United States Confronts the World *(Lynne Reinner Publishers), is now available.*

Washington finally realizes after its chronic troop shortage in Iraq and elsewhere that Defense Secretary Donald Rumsfeld's vision of quickly 'shocking and awing' enemies to win victories has been spectacularly unsuccessful, and that the United States needs foreign manpower more desperately than ever. Its global visions – and illusions – cannot be attained without them. These visions involve a 'long war' against largely undefined, elusive terrorists and enemies in every corner of the globe for decades to come. Hence its renewed emphasis in its *Quadrennial Defense Review*, released this February, on Nato and mobilizing foreign troops 'to share the risks and responsibilities of today's complex challenges.'

Washington now favours a rapprochement with 'old Europe' and the nations it dismissed after September 11, 2001, and it wants to build a 'strategic consensus' and to expand Nato's role notwithstanding its resolution after the 1999 war in the former Yugoslavia to never again allow Nato's consensual voting procedures to constrain American actions – as, indeed, it has not. Its belief in the sufficiency of 'coalitions of the willing,' to cite Rumsfeld's words, has proven to be a chimera. In this regard, the Bush Administration now tacitly admits that its view after 2001 that it could pursue its global role alone was a colossal failure. The immense pressures to send troops to Afghanistan it imposed on The Netherlands reflects this desire to resuscitate and expand the Nato system.

The United States' 'ambitious agenda' was outlined by the US ambassador to Nato (and former aide to Cheney) Victoria Nuland's interview in the January 24 *Financial Times*. The US wants a 'globally deployable military force' that will operate everywhere – from Africa to the Middle East and beyond. It will include Japan and Australia as well as the Nato nations. 'It's a totally different animal,' to quote her, whose ultimate role will be subject to

United States desires and adventures. Nato must have a '...common collective deployment at strategic distances.' Troops to Afghanistan are largely symbolic, a secondary issue to the much more important question of Nato's future in American calculations over coming years. Nato, which was originally to be a European-focused alliance, would now become global in scope.

The official Munich conference on security policy in early February 2006 – which Rumsfeld attended along with Brent Scowcroft, former Defense Secretary William Cohen, and other advocates of the traditional Atlantic alliance – reflected the American desire to transform Nato so it will again be a useful weapon in its sheath of military choices – particularly its manpower. This is all the more essential because his plans for reforming the entire military will lead to a 20 per cent reduction of manoeuvre battalions in favour of larger headquarters and more high tech weapons, and soldiers on the ground will be scarcer than ever. It also wants the Nato states to spend more on their military forces, thereby relieving the United States from increasing its already huge budget deficit.

The Bush Administration's ambitions for Nato are based on more ideological neo-con fantasies which must not be encouraged. The same American leaders have ignored their own intelligence to pursue ambitions which have traumatized Afghanistan and the Middle East, and today threaten the peace elsewhere. If its schemes for Nato that Nuland outlines gain the support of European states, then the United States is likely to commit more follies and create unforeseen miseries to fulfil its illusions.

American objectives – beyond fighting a war on 'terror' – are inherently indefinable as to length and location, but certain to be very ambitious. Fear is the adhesive that creates alliances and keeps them together, and the fear of Communism and the Soviet Union that led to Nato's creation has been replaced by the fear of Muslim fundamentalism, terrorism, and the like. But just as the dangers of Communism proved illusory, so, too, will American threats of universal terror and chaos also prove to be a myth. The problem is what the United States will do before its allies grow tired of its paranoid politics. It has already said it wants Nato to send more troops to Kosovo so that it can ship 1700 American soldiers there to Iraq. The Netherlands has agreed to its demand on sending forces to Afghanistan, but it and all Nato members have to prepare for more troop requests in the future as part of 'ambitious' unilateralist Washington goals everywhere. That is the central issue that the Nato members must now confront.

The Nato contingents now in Afghanistan will not succeed where the Americans have already failed after four years to build a state no longer controlled by warlords, drug lords, and various Islamic fundamentalists. They will be shot at and killed, and the publics of the Nato states will become increasingly anti-war and vote out of office those who have obeyed American advice. They have already done so in Spain, they may do the same in Italy, and while Washington may win in the short run, ultimately there is a very good chance that its successes will produce a crisis in Nato – and perhaps the end of this organizational artifact of the Cold War.

In a word, we are at the beginning, not the end, of a profound crisis in US relations with The Netherlands and other Nato members. European nations may now articulate a political identity that is both in their national interests and conforms to their values – the very thing that the United States hoped Nato would prevent from occurring when it created it over a half-century ago. The Bush Administration may very well compel them to become more independent. That is to be welcomed.

TRANSPORT & GENERAL WORKERS' UNION
London, South East & East Anglia

Join the March on May Day
TRADE UNION FREEDOM BILL
Clerkenwell Green to Trafalgar Square

Forward to employment law that gives guaranteed rights and freedoms fully compliant with international labour standards

Barry Camfield
Asst. Gen. Secretary

John Aitkin
Regional Chair

(phone)
020. 8800. 4281

Web
www.tgwu.org.uk

(fax)
020. 8802. 8388

Regime Change in Iran

For the first time in print the secret CIA history of the overthrow of Premier Mossadeq of Iran.

In 1953, a *coup d'état* in Iran was carefully organised by the Central Intelligence Agency of the US together with the British Secret Intelligence Service.

This publication provides a short guide through the labyrinths of the world where things are not what they seem to be. Yet, the parallels to the current confrontation with Iran are all too clear.

Price: £8.99 including p&p

Spokesman Books, Russell House, Bulwell Lane, Nottingham, NG6 0BT, England
Tel: 0115 9708318 - Fax: 0115 9420433
Credit/Debit cards welcome
elfeuro@compuserve.com
www.spokesmanbooks.com

War in Iraq: Time to Go!

The Honorable John P. Murtha

Congressman Murtha has followed long service in the US Marine Corps with more than 30 years in the United States House of Representatives. We reproduce in full his devastating call of November 2005 to 'bring the troops home'.

'One person with whom the Pentagon's top commanders have shared their private views for decades is Representative John Murtha, of Pennsylvania, the senior Democrat on the House Defense Appropriations Subcommittee. The President and his key aides were enraged when, on November 17th, Murtha gave a speech in the House calling for a withdrawal of troops within six months. The speech was filled with devastating information.'

Seymour Hersh, The New Yorker

* * *

The war in Iraq is not going as advertised. It is a flawed policy wrapped in illusion. The American public is way ahead of us. The United States and coalition troops have done all they can in Iraq, but it is time for a change in direction. Our military is suffering. The future of our country is at risk. We cannot continue on the present course. It is evident that continued military action in Iraq is not in the best interest of the United States of America, the Iraqi people or the Persian Gulf Region.

General Casey said in a September 2005 Hearing, 'the perception of occupation in Iraq is a major driving force behind the insurgency.' General Abizaid said on the same date, 'Reducing the size and visibility of the coalition forces in Iraq is a part of our counterinsurgency strategy.'

For two-and-a-half years I have been concerned about the United States policy and the plan in Iraq. I have addressed my concerns with the Administration and the Pentagon and have spoken out in public about my concerns. The main reason for going to war has been discredited. A few days before the start of the war I was in Kuwait – the military drew a red line around Baghdad and said when US forces cross that line they will be attacked by the Iraqis with weapons of mass destruction – but the US forces said they were prepared. They had well trained forces with the appropriate protective gear.

We spend more money on intelligence than all the countries in the world together, and more on intelligence than most countries' gross domestic product. But the intelligence concerning Iraq was wrong. It is not a world intelligence failure. It is a United States intelligence failure and the way that intelligence was misused.

I have been visiting our wounded troops at Bethesda and Walter Reed hospitals almost every week since the beginning of the War. And what demoralizes them is going to war with not enough troops and equipment to make the transition to peace; the devastation caused by improvised explosive devices; being deployed to Iraq when their homes have been ravaged by hurricanes; being on their second or third deployment and leaving their families behind without a network of support.

The threat posed by terrorism is real, but we have other threats that cannot be ignored. We must be prepared to face all threats. The future of our military is at risk. Our military and their families are stretched thin. Many say that the Army is broken. Some of our troops are on their third deployment. Recruitment is down, even as our military has lowered its standards. Defence budgets are being cut. Personnel costs are skyrocketing, particularly in health care. Choices will have to be made. We cannot allow promises we have made to our military families in terms of service benefits, in terms of their health care, to be negotiated away. Procurement programmes that ensure our military dominance cannot be negotiated away. We must be prepared. The war in Iraq has caused huge shortfalls at our bases in the United States.

Much of our ground equipment is worn out and in need of either serious overhaul or replacement. George Washington said, 'To be prepared for war is one of the most effective means of preserving peace.' We must rebuild our Army. Our deficit is growing out of control. The Director of the Congressional Budget Office recently admitted to being 'terrified' about the budget deficit in the coming decades. This is the first prolonged war we have fought with three years of tax cuts, without full mobilization of American industry and without a draft. The burden of this war has not been shared equally; the military and their families are shouldering this burden.

Our military has been fighting a war in Iraq for over two and-a-half years. Our military has accomplished its mission and done its duty. Our military captured Saddam Hussein, and captured or killed his closest associates. But the war continues to intensify. Deaths and injuries are growing, with over 2,079 confirmed American deaths. Over 15,500 have been seriously injured and it is estimated that over 50,000 will suffer from battle fatigue. There have been reports of at least 30,000 Iraqi civilian deaths.

I just recently visited Anbar Province in Iraq in order to assess the conditions on the ground. Last May 2005, as part of the Emergency Supplemental Spending Bill, the House included the Moran Amendment, which was accepted in Conference, and which required the Secretary of Defense to submit quarterly reports to Congress in order to more accurately measure stability and security in

Iraq. We have now received two reports. I am disturbed by the findings in key indicator areas. Oil production and energy production are below pre-war levels. Our reconstruction efforts have been crippled by the security situation. Only $9 billion of the $18 billion appropriated for reconstruction has been spent. Unemployment remains at about 60 per cent. Clean water is scarce. Only $500 million of the $2.2 billion appropriated for water projects has been spent. And most importantly, insurgent incidents have increased from about 150 per week to over 700 in the last year. Instead of attacks going down over time and with the addition of more troops, attacks have grown dramatically. Since the revelations at Abu Ghraib, American casualties have doubled. An annual State Department report in 2004 indicated a sharp increase in global terrorism.

I said over a year ago, and now the military and the Administration agrees, Iraq cannot be won 'militarily.' I said two years ago, the key to progress in Iraq is to Iraqitize, Internationalize and Energize. I believe the same today. But I have concluded that the presence of US troops in Iraq is impeding this progress.

Our troops have become the primary target of the insurgency. They are united against US forces and we have become a catalyst for violence. US troops are the common enemy of the Sunnis, Saddamists and foreign jihadists. I believe with a US troop redeployment, the Iraqi security forces will be incentivized to take control. A poll recently conducted shows that over 80 per cent of Iraqis are strongly opposed to the presence of coalition troops, and about 45 per cent of the Iraqi population believe attacks against American troops are justified. I believe we need to turn Iraq over to the Iraqis. I believe before the Iraqi elections, scheduled for mid-December, the Iraqi people and the emerging government must be put on notice that the United States will immediately redeploy. All of Iraq must know that Iraq is free. Free from United States occupation. I believe this will send a signal to the Sunnis to join the political process for the good of a 'free' Iraq.

My plan calls:
To immediately redeploy US troops consistent with the safety of US forces.
To create a quick reaction force in the region.
To create an over-the-horizon presence of Marines.
To diplomatically pursue security and stability in Iraq

This war needs to be personalized. As I said before, I have visited with the severely wounded of this war. They are suffering.

Because we in Congress are charged with sending our sons and daughters into battle, it is our responsibility, our *obligation*, to speak out for them. That's why I am speaking out.

Our military has done everything that has been asked of them. The United States cannot accomplish anything further in Iraq militarily. *It is time to bring them home.*

Christopher Hampton – Three Poems

PROLOGUE TO WAR

'The kaleidoscope has been shaken. The pieces are in flux. Soon they will settle again. Before they do, let us re-order this world around us.'
Tony Blair, Labour Party Conference Speech, 2nd October 2001

This is what transcendence does to us.
It brings about the triumph of the cloaked,
the invisible, the unaccountable,
over that which can be brought to book.
Things driven by the god-obsessed
and their so-called godless enemies
sweep aside the human context
even as the hidden hand of profit does.
Now, with the moral order of the West
assuming beneficent control of the just
against the absolutes of Islam,
the politics of transcendence float above
the brutal politics of hatred and death.
And how are we to treat this high-altitude
language of the liberal conscience pitting
compassion against force, and telling us,
even as the bombers move in on Kabul,
'the values we believe in should shine through
whatever we do in Afghanistan.'

THE IMPERATIVES OF PROMISE

So take it up again. What waits in silence
through the tragedies of history, in the broken mists,
beyond the doorstep, out below the planets,
where the questions beckon, is the key: the word-game.
Play it cool, play deep, play hard, make patterns
count in the thrust of dispute and disjunction;
bring together what in a century of betrayals
pulls apart – these broken imperatives of promise
that have driven millions to crisis and despair.
It's not an option. There are words that cross the frontiers
of hope and failure, to challenge the violence

that isolates and make it possible to act
against the operators of the killer-systems
we have helped to put in place. And what they start from
is refusal, stubbornness of quest, insistence
on the fundamentals of distinction by which
fuses are lit that might begin to bring back light
to a darkened and damaged universe.

ROSA LUXEMBURG AT WRONKE

October 1916 until July 1917

To be free to think and dream
as she walks the rain
in Madam Kautsky's cloak.
To feel as much at home
with the green of her plants
as ever she'd been on the battlefield
of European politics.
The world was there with her of course –
that murderous world
she'd walked the tightrope of
through all the jugglings of expediency,
up to the edge with the SPD
and its war-credit sell-out.

Listen! When I get back
there'll be no more meetings,
clandestine or otherwise!
I'll take my stand
in the thick of the action
where the wind roars in the ears.
I've had enough of talking.
What we need's commitment,
getting at the roots, making things new!

Now though it's back to my plants!

Christopher Hampton is the author of The Ideology of the Text *and editor of* A Radical Reader: The struggle for change in England 1381-1914 (*Spokesman Books, forthcoming*). *These poems are from his latest collection,* Border Crossings *(Katabasis Press).*

I WANTED ALL
THINGS TO SEEM TO
MAKE SOME SENSE,
SO WE COULD ALL BE
HAPPY, YES, INSTEAD
OF TENSE. AND I
MADE UP LIES, SO
THEY ALL FIT NICE,
AND I MADE THIS
SAD WORLD A
PARADISE.

Dispatch from a Man without a Country

Kurt Vonnegut

Kurt Vonnegut's latest book is A Man without a Country *(Bloomsbury), from which this excerpt is taken by kind permission of the author.*

Do you know what a twerp is? When I was in Shortridge High School in Indianapolis 65 years ago, a twerp was a guy who stuck a set of false teeth up his butt and bit the buttons off the back seats of taxicabs. (And a snarf was a guy who sniffed the seats of girls' bicycles.)

And I consider anybody a twerp who hasn't read the greatest American short story, which is 'Occurrence at Owl Creek Bridge,' by Ambrose Bierce. It isn't remotely political. It is a flawless example of American genius, like 'Sophisticated Lady' by Duke Ellington or the Franklin stove.

I consider anybody a twerp who hasn't read *Democracy in America* by Alexis de Tocqueville. There can never be a better book than that one on the strengths and vulnerabilities inherent in our form of government.

Want a taste of that great book? He says, and he said it 169 years ago, that in no country other than ours has a love of money taken a stronger hold on the affections of men. Okay?

The French-Algerian writer Albert Camus, who won a Nobel Prize for Literature in 1957, wrote, 'There is but one truly serious philosophical problem, and that is suicide.'

So there's another barrel of laughs from literature. Camus died in an automobile accident. His dates? 1913 – 1960 A.D.

Do you realize that all great literature – *Moby Dick, Huckleberry Finn, A Farewell to Arms, The Scarlet Letter, The Red Badge of Courage, The Iliad and The Odyssey, Crime and Punishment, The Bible, and* 'The Charge of the Light Brigade' – are all about what a bummer it is to be a human being? (Isn't it such a relief to have somebody say that?)

Evolution can go to hell as far as I am concerned. What a mistake we are. We have mortally wounded this sweet life-supporting planet – the only one in the whole Milky Way – with a century of transportation whoopee. Our government is conducting a war against drugs, is it? Let them go after petroleum. Talk about a destructive high! You put some of this stuff in your car and you can go a hundred miles an hour, run over the neighbor's dog, and tear the atmosphere to smithereens. Hey, as long as we are stuck with being homo sapiens, why mess around? Let's wreck the whole joint. Anybody got an atomic bomb? Who doesn't have an atomic bomb nowadays?

But I have to say this in defense of humankind: In no matter what era in history, including the Garden of Eden, everybody just got here. And, except for the Garden of Eden, there were already all these games going on that could make you act crazy, even if you weren't crazy to begin with. Some of the crazymaking games going on today are love and hate, liberalism and conservatism, automobiles and credit cards, golf, and girls' basketball.

I am one of America's Great Lakes people, her freshwater people, not an oceanic but a continental people. Whenever I swim in an ocean, I feel as though I am swimming in chicken soup.

Like me, many American socialists were freshwater people. Most American people don't know what the socialists did during the first half of the past century with art, with eloquence, with organizing skills, to elevate the self-respect, the dignity and political acumen of American wage earners of our working class.

That wage earners, without social position or higher education or wealth, are of inferior intellect is surely belied by the fact that two of the most splendid writers and speakers on the deepest subject in American history were self-taught workmen. I speak, of course, of Carl Sandburg the poet from Illinois, and Abraham Lincoln of Kentucky, then Indiana, and finally Illinois. Both, may I say, were continental, freshwater people like me. Another freshwater person and splendid speaker was the Socialist Party candidate Eugene Victor Debs, a former locomotive fireman who had been born to a middle class family in Terra Haute, Indiana.

Hooray for our team!

'Socialism' is no more an evil word than 'Christianity.' Socialism no more prescribed Joseph Stalin and his secret police and shuttered churches than Christianity prescribed the Spanish Inquisition. Christianity and socialism alike, in fact, prescribe a society dedicated to the proposition that all men, women and children are created equal and shall not starve.

Adolf Hitler, incidentally, was a two-fer. He named his party the National Socialists, the Nazis. Hitler's swastika wasn't a pagan symbol, as so many people believe. It was a working person's Christian cross, made of axes, of tools.

About Stalin's shuttered churches, and those in China today: Such suppression of religion was supposedly justified by Karl Marx's statement that 'religion is the opium of the people.' Marx said that back in 1844, when opium and opium derivatives were the only effective painkillers anyone could take. Marx himself had taken them. He was grateful for the temporary relief they had given him. He was simply noticing, and surely not condemning, the fact that religion could also be comforting to those in economic or social distress. It was a casual truism, not a dictum.

When Marx wrote those words, by the way, we hadn't even freed our slaves yet. Who do you imagine was more pleasing in the eyes of a merciful God back then, Karl Marx or the United States of America?

Stalin was happy to take Marx's truism as a decree, and Chinese tyrants as well, since it seemingly empowered them to put preachers out of business who might speak ill of them or their goals.

The statement has also entitled many of this country to say that socialists are antireligion, are anti-God, and therefore absolutely loathsome.

I never met Carl Sandburg or Eugene Victor Debs, and I wish I had. I would have been tongue-tied in the presence of such national treasures.

I did get to know one socialist of their generation – Powers Hapgood of Indianapolis. He was a typical Hoosier idealist. Socialism is idealistic. Hapgood, like Debs, was a middle-class person who thought there could be more economic justice in this country. He wanted a better country, that's all.

After graduating from Harvard, he went to work as a coal miner, urging his working class brothers to organize in order to get better pay and safer working conditions. He also led protesters at the execution of the anarchists Nicola Sacco and Bartolomeo Vanzetti in Massachusetts in 1927.

Hapgood's family owned a successful cannery in Indianapolis, and when Powers Hapgood inherited it, he turned it over to the employees, who ruined it.

We met in Indianapolis after the end of the Second World War. He had become an official in the CIO. There had been some sort of dust-up on a picket line, and he was testifying about it in court, and the judge stops everything and asks him, 'Mr Hapgood, here you are, you're a graduate of Harvard. Why would anyone with your advantages choose to live as you have?' Hapgood answered the judge: 'Why, because of the Sermon on the Mount, sir.'

And again: Hooray for our team.

I am from a family of artists. Here I am, making a living in the arts. It has not been a rebellion. It's as though I had taken over the family Esso station. My ancestors were all in the arts, so I'm simply making my living in the customary family way.

But my father, who was a painter and an architect, was so hurt by the Depression, when he was unable to make a living, that he thought I should have nothing to do with the arts. He warned me away from the arts because he had found them so useless as a way of producing money. He told me I could go to college only if I studied something serious, something practical.

As an undergraduate at Cornell I was a chemistry major because my brother was a big-shot chemist. Critics feel that a person cannot be a serious artist and also have had a technical education, which I had. I know that customarily English departments in universities, without knowing what they're doing, teach dread of the engineering department, the physics department, and the chemistry department. And this fear, I think, is carried over into criticism. Most of our critics are products of English departments and are very suspicious of anyone who takes an interest in technology. So, anyway, I was a chemistry major, but I'm always winding up as a teacher in English departments, so I have brought scientific thinking to literature. There's been very little gratitude for this.

I became a so-called science fiction writer when someone decreed that I was a science fiction writer. I did not want to be classified as one, so I wondered in what way I'd offended that I would not get credit for being a serious writer. I decided that it was because I wrote about technology, and most fine American writers know nothing about technology. I got classified as a science fiction writer simply because I wrote about Schenectady, New York. My first book, *Player Piano*, was about Schenectady. There are huge factories in Schenectady and nothing else. I and my associates were engineers, physicists, chemists, and mathematicians. And when I wrote about the General Electric Company and Schenectady, it seemed a fantasy of the future to critics who had never seen the place.

I think that novels that leave out technology misrepresent life as badly as Victorians misrepresented life by leaving out sex.

In 1968, the year I wrote *Slaughterhouse Five*, I finally became grown up enough to write about the bombing of Dresden. It was the largest massacre in European history. I, of course, know about Auschwitz, but a massacre is something that happens suddenly, the killing of a whole lot of people in a very short time. In Dresden, on February 13, 1945, about 135,000 people were killed by British firebombing in one night.

It was pure nonsense, pointless destruction. The whole city was burned down, and it was a British atrocity, not ours. They sent in night bombers, and they came in and set the whole town on fire with a new kind of incendiary bomb. And so everything organic, except my little POW group, was consumed by fire. It was a military experiment to find out if you could burn down a whole city by scattering incendiaries over it.

Of course, as prisoners of war, we dealt hands-on with dead Germans, digging them out of basements because they had suffocated there, and taking them to a huge funeral pyre. And I heard – I didn't see it done – that they gave up this procedure because it was too slow and, of course, the city was starting to smell pretty bad. And they sent in guys with flamethrowers.

Why my fellow prisoners of war and I weren't killed I don't know.

I was a writer in 1968. I was a hack. I'd write anything to make money, you know. And what the hell, I'd seen this thing. I'd been through it, and so I was going to write a hack book about Dresden. You know, the kind that would be made into a movie and where Dean Martin and Frank Sinatra and the others would play us. I tried to write, but I just couldn't get it right. I kept writing crap.

So I went to a friend's house – Bernie O'Hare, who'd been my pal. And we were trying to remember funny stuff about our time as prisoners of war in Dresden, tough talk and all that, stuff that would make a nifty war movie. And his wife, Mary O'Hare, blew her stack. She said, 'You were nothing but babies then.'

And that is true of soldiers. They are in fact babies. They are not movie stars. They are not Duke Wayne. And realizing that was the key. I was finally free to tell the truth. We were children and the subtitle of *Slaughterhouse Five* became *The Children's Crusade*.

Why had it taken me twenty-three years to write about what I had experienced in Dresden? We all came home with stories, and we all wanted to cash in, one way or another. And what Mary O'Hare was saying, in effect, was, 'Why don't you tell the truth for a change?'

Ernest Hemingway wrote a story after the First World War called 'A Soldier's Home' about how it was very rude to ask a soldier what he'd seen when he got back home. I think a lot of people, including me, clammed up when a civilian asked about battle, about war. It was fashionable. One of the most impressive ways to tell your war story is to refuse to tell it, you know. Civilians would then have to imagine all kinds of deeds of derring-do.

But I think the Vietnam War freed me and other writers, because it made our leadership and our motives seem so scruffy and essentially stupid. We could finally talk about something bad that we did to the worst people imaginable, the Nazis. And what I saw, what I had to report, made war look so ugly. You know, the truth can be really powerful stuff. You're not expecting it.

Of course, another reason not to talk about war is that it's unspeakable.

FUNNIEST JOKE IN THE WORLD: "LAST NIGHT I DREAMED I WAS EATING FLANNEL CAKES. WHEN I WOKE UP THE BLANKET WAS GONE!"

Here is a lesson in creative writing.

First rule: Do not use semicolons. They are transvestite hermaphrodites representing absolutely nothing. All they do is show you've been to college.

And I realize some of you may be having trouble deciding whether I'm kidding or not. So from now on I will tell you when I'm kidding.

For instance, join the National Guard or the Marines and teach democracy. I'm kidding.

We are about to be attacked by Al Qaeda. Wave flags if you have them. That always seems to scare them away. I'm kidding.

If you want to really hurt your parents, and you don't have the nerve to be gay, the least you can do is go into the arts. I'm not kidding. The arts are not a way to make a living. They are a very human way of making life more bearable. Practising an art, no matter how well or badly, is a way to make your soul grow, for heaven's sake. Sing in the shower. Dance to the radio. Tell stories. Write a poem to a friend, even a lousy poem. Do it as well as you possibly can. You will get an enormous reward. You will have created something.

I want to share with you something I've learned. I'll draw it on the blackboard behind me so you can follow more easily [*draws a vertical line on the blackboard*]. This is the G-I axis: good fortune – ill fortune. Death and terrible poverty, sickness down here – great prosperity, wonderful health up there. Your average state of affairs in the middle [*points to bottom, top, and middle of line respectively*].

This is the B-E axis. B for beginning, E for entropy. Okay. Not every story has that very simple, very pretty shape that even a computer can understand [*draws horizontal line extending from middle of G-I axis*].

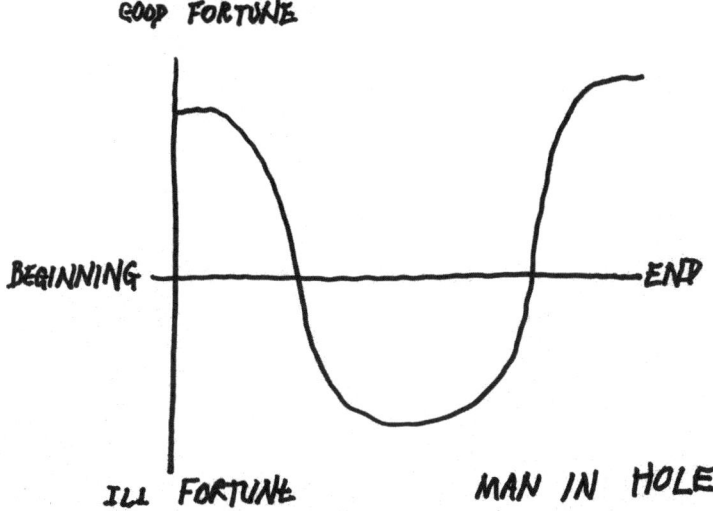

Now let me give you a marketing tip. The people who can afford to buy books and magazines and go to the movies don't like to hear about people who are poor or sick, so start your story up here [*indicates top of the G-I axis*]. You will see this story over and over again. People love it and it is not copyrighted. The story is 'Man in Hole,' but the story needn't be about a man or a hole. It's: Somebody gets into trouble, gets out of it again [*draws line A*]. It is not accidental that the line ends up higher than where it began. This is encouraging to readers.

Another is called 'Boy Meets Girl,' but this needn't be about a boy meeting a girl [*begins drawing line B*]. It's: Somebody, an ordinary person, on a day like any other day, comes across something perfectly wonderful: 'Oh boy, this is my lucky day!' ... [*drawing the line downward*]. 'Shit!' ... [*drawing the line back up again*] And gets back up again.

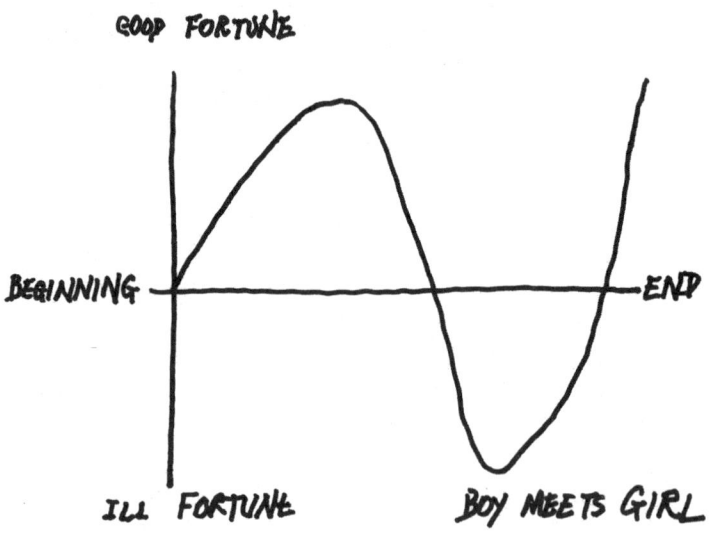

Now, I don't mean to intimidate you, but after being a chemist as an undergraduate at Cornell, after the war I went to the University of Chicago and studied anthropology, and eventually I took a masters degree in that field. Saul Bellow was in that same department, and neither one of us ever made a field trip. Although we certainly imagined some. I started going to the library in search of reports about ethnographers, preachers, and explorers – those imperialists – to find out what sorts of stories they'd collected from primitive people. It was a big mistake for me to take a degree in anthropology anyway, because I can't stand primitive people – they're so stupid. But anyway, I read these stories, one after another, collected from primitive people all over the world, and they were dead level, like the B-E axis here. So all right. Primitive people deserve to lose with their lousy stories. They really are backward. Look at the wonderful rise and fall of our stories.

One of the most popular stories ever told starts down here [*begins line C below*

B-E axis]. Who is this person who's despondent? She's a girl of about fifteen or sixteen whose mother has died, so why wouldn't she be low? And her father got married almost immediately to a terrible battle-axe with two mean daughters. You've heard it?

There's to be a party at the palace. She has to help her two stepsisters and her dreadful stepmother get ready to go, but she herself has to stay home. Is she even sadder now? No, she's already a broken-hearted little girl. The death of her mother is enough. Things can't get any worse than that. So okay, they all leave for the party. Her fairy godmother shows up [*draws incremental rise*], gives her pantyhose, mascara, and a means of transportation to get to the party.

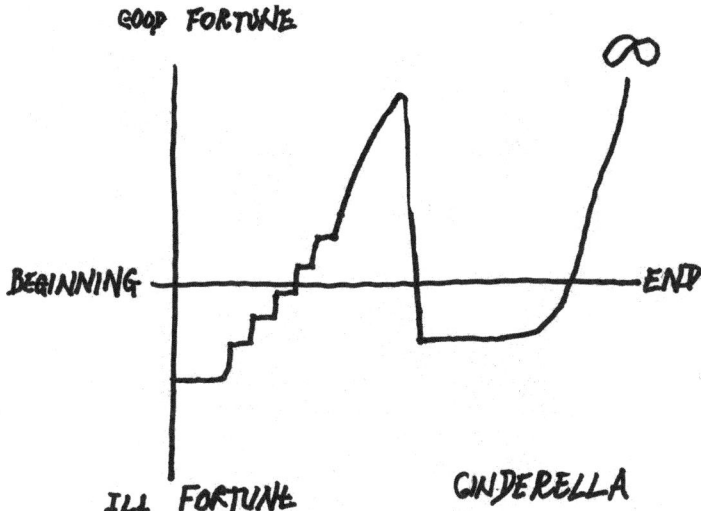

CINDERELLA

And when she shows up she's the belle of the ball [*draws line upward*]. She is so heavily made up that her relatives don't recognize her. Then the clock strikes twelve, as promised, and it's all taken away again [*draws line downward*]. It doesn't take long for a clock to strike twelve times, so she drops down. Does she drop down to the same level? Hell, no. No matter what happens after that she'll remember when the prince was in love with her and she was the belle of the ball. So she poops along, at her considerably improved level, no matter what, and the shoe fits, and she becomes off-scale happy [*draws line upward and then infinity symbol*].

Now there's a Franz Kafka story [*begins line D towards bottom of G-I axis*]. A young man is rather unattractive and not very personable. He has disagreeable relatives and has had a lot of jobs with no chance of promotion. He doesn't get paid enough to take his girl dancing or to go to the beer hall with a friend. One morning he wakes up, it's time to go to work again, and he has turned into a cockroach [*draws line downward and then infinity symbol*]. It's a pessimistic story.

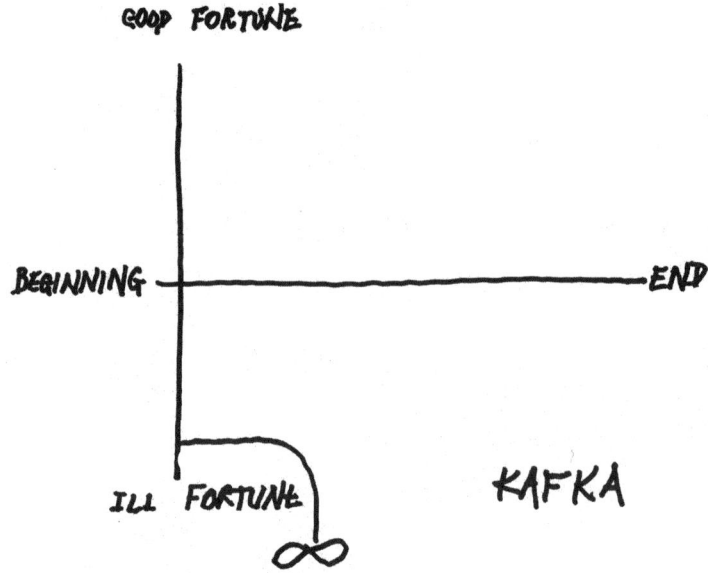

The question is, does this system I've devised help us in the evaluation of literature? Perhaps a real masterpiece cannot be crucified on a cross of this design. How about *Hamlet*? It's a pretty good piece of work I'd say. Is anybody going to argue that it isn't? I don't have to draw a new line, because Hamlet's situation is the same as Cinderella's, except that the sexes are reversed.

His father has just died. He's despondent. And right away his mother went and married his uncle, who's a bastard. So Hamlet is going along on the same level as Cinderella when his friend Horatio comes up to him and says, 'Hamlet, listen there's this thing up in the parapet, I think maybe you'd better talk to it. It's your dad.' So Hamlet goes up and talks to this, you know, fairly substantial apparition there. And this thing says, 'I'm your father, I was murdered, you gotta avenge me, it was your uncle did it, here's how.'

Well, was this good news or bad news? To this day we don't know if that ghost was really Hamlet's father. If you have messed around with Ouija boards, you know there are malicious spirits floating around, liable to tell you anything, and you shouldn't believe them. Madame Blavatsky, who knew more about the spirit world than anybody else, said you are a fool to take any apparition seriously, because they are often malicious and they are frequently the souls of people who were murdered, were suicides, or were terribly cheated in life in one way or another, and they are out for revenge.

So we don't know whether this thing was really Hamlet's father or if it was good news or bad news. And neither does Hamlet. But he says okay, I got a way to check this out. I'll hire actors to act out the way the ghost said my father was murdered by my uncle, and I'll put on this show and see what my uncle makes of it. So he puts on this show. And it's not like Perry Mason. His uncle doesn't go crazy and say, 'I-I-You got me, you got me, I did it, I did it.' It flops. Neither good news nor bad news. After this flop Hamlet ends up talking with his mother when the drapes move, so he thinks his uncle is back there and he says, 'All right, I am so sick of being so damn indecisive,' and he sticks his rapier through the drapery. Well, who falls out? This windbag, Polonius. This Rush Limbaugh. And Shakespeare regards him as a fool and quite disposable.

You know, dumb parents think that the advice that Polonius gave to his kids when they were going away was what parents should always tell their kids, and it's the dumbest possible advice, and Shakespeare even thought it was hilarious.

'Neither a borrower nor a lender be.' But what else is life but endless lending and borrowing, give and take?

'This above all, to thin own self be true.' Be an egomaniac!

Neither good news nor bad news. Hamlet didn't get arrested. He's prince. He can kill anybody he wants. So he goes along, and finally he gets in a duel, and he's killed. Well, did he go to heaven or did he go to hell? Quite a difference. Cinderella or Kafka's cockroach? I don't think Shakespeare believed in a heaven or hell any more than I do. And so we don't know whether it's good news or bad news.

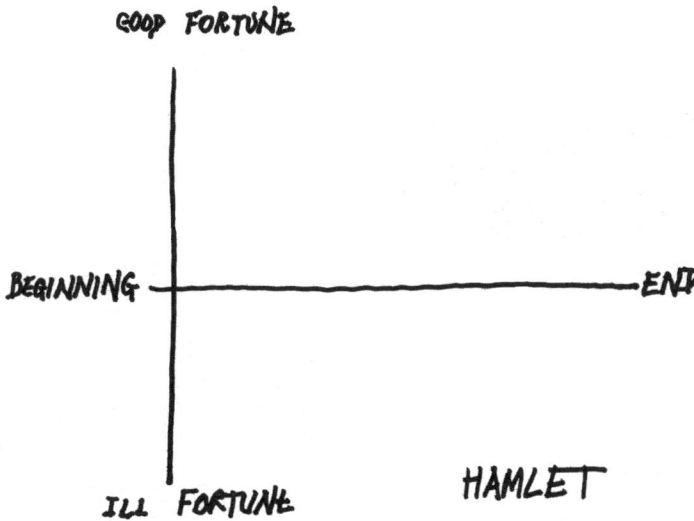

I have just demonstrated to you that Shakespeare was as poor a storyteller as any Arapaho.

But there's a reason we recognize *Hamlet* as a masterpiece: it's that Shakespeare told us the truth, and people so rarely tell us the truth in this rise and fall here [*indicates blackboard*]. The truth is, we know so little about life, we don't really know what the good news is and what the bad news is.

And if I die – God forbid – I would like to go to heaven to ask somebody in charge up there, 'Hey, what was the good news and what was the bad news?'

UN: Quis custodiet ipsos custodes?

Denis Halliday interviewed by David Barsamian

Denis Halliday worked for the United Nations for more than 30 years. He rose to the rank of Assistant Secretary General. In the late 1990s, he was the UN's Humanitarian Coordinator in Iraq. He resigned his position in protest at the continuing economic sanctions against the country and the harm they were doing to the Iraqi people.

David Barsamian is the Director of Alternative Radio (www.alternativeradio.org), based in Boulder, Colorado in the United States. His latest books are Imperial Ambitions *with Noam Chomsky and* Speaking of Empire and Resistance *with Tariq Ali.*

David Barsamian spoke with Denis Halliday in Istanbul in June 2005, during the proceedings of the World Tribunal on Iraq. His questions and comments are printed in italic text, and Mr Halliday's replies appear in ordinary text.

One of the arguments that the Bush administration has made since its invasion of Iraq is that many people were against the sanctions, they were punitive and caused great harm to the Iraqi people. And now, because of regime change in Baghdad, people should be happy the sanctions have ended.

I'm sure the Iraqis would have been happy that the sanctions had ended, and we all would have recognized that, if the occupation had been handled correctly and properly, and if the needs of the Iraqi people had been taken care of, under the obligations of occupation as defined by international law. But that has been a total failure. We now see child mortality and malnutrition on the increase in Iraq. We see almost a complete breakdown in law and order and the social and educational and health activities and needs of the Iraqi civilian population. It's worse now than it was under sanctions.

Another argument that is frequently heard is that Iraq is better off without Saddam Hussein. What is your response to that?

That's an interesting question. But the United States has no right to make that decision. That's a decision for the people of Iraq. And had we lifted sanctions ten years ago, and had the people of Iraq been given the chance to live their lives and have their employment and look after their children and all the basic needs that we take care of for ourselves, I think they might have made the same decision, and they might have overthrown Saddam Hussein. People think that's unreasonable. But then I point them to Indonesia—Suharto, a genuine general (not like Saddam Hussein) who controlled Indonesia, a country of 200 million people, through his military power. He was overthrown by a student movement, and the loss of life was a handful. I think the Iraqis would have done the same had we given them the capacity to do so.

What about the historical precedents? In 1945, the Allies convened a tribunal in Nuremberg which convicted high-ranking German state and military officials for the crime of aggressive war, for launching unprovoked attacks on different countries. That Nuremberg principle is then encoded in the United Nations Charter.

I would have said that the International Criminal Court, in a sense, is a substitute for a Nuremberg-Tokyo situation, because the Court requires domestic prosecution. So the right way to deal with a Clinton or an Albright or a Bush is impeachment, to use the powers that exist under domestic law in the United States and under the Constitution. Likewise with Tony Blair. It's only when that fails that we should go to international prosecution. It can't be the International Criminal Court for the past. It can be the International Criminal Court for the future. And in the case of the United States, the Court could operate with Bush *in absentia*, given his reluctance and fear of international law.

I think the Nuremberg process is wrong in the sense that the war crimes were committed on both sides. They're not justifiable. Whether you fire-bomb Hamburg and kill 100,000, or you drop, as Truman did, the weapons on Hiroshima and Nagasaki, those also are war crimes. And the trial of Nuremberg should have encompassed all those who acted in breach of law.

Goering, the highest-ranking Nazi on trial, said it was victors' justice.

He, of course, was right. And that's 1945. We're doing it again. We're now so ready to prosecute those who lose, but when we win, somehow we believe we are above international law. And that I find extraordinary.

In the period leading up to the attack on Iraq, the American public was subjected to a steady stream of warnings from the Bush administration about the 'unique' nature of the Iraqi threat, the 'growing' danger it posed. Cheney said there was 'no doubt' that Iraq had weapons of mass destruction. Tony Blair added to the chorus for war saying Iraq could launch weapons in 'forty-five minutes'. How were they able to convince large numbers of people that these claims were true?

They had access to a massive propaganda machine. They're artists of spin. They employ people to mislead and misinform. They're into propaganda on a massive scale we've never seen, perhaps, before. And the access that Tony Blair and George Bush had to the media is extraordinary. And those of us, many millions, who were opposed, horrified by what seemed to be about to happen, really had very little access except through alternative media outlets and the internet. It's not difficult, it seems to me, to convince a population when you build on these fears and you mislead and you misinform.

We know perfectly well that Iraq was not a threat to the United States or to Britain. The neighbourhood, the Kuwaitis and the Saudis, even up to the end of 2002, were very slow to endorse the Bush approach. They did not recognize that they were threatened by the very limited capacity available to Saddam Hussein at that stage, by the end of 2002. This is a fiction which was sold very clearly by the artists of spin in Washington and London.

Central to selling the war was Secretary of State Colin Powell's presentation at the United Nations on 5 February 2003. He made more than twenty allegations about Iraq, ranging from mobile weapons launchers to Scud missiles to underground factory labs. He held up a vial saying that this amount of anthrax could wipe out large numbers of people. His speech got a rather tepid response from the UN audience. But the US media regarded it as a magisterial performance, one of the greatest examples of diplomacy in memory.

We all watched it, and most of us felt it was an extraordinary example of misinformation. And disappointing, because I think many of us hoped that within the Bush administration, Mr. Powell was perhaps one of the very few who was a man of integrity and would follow the right path. Clearly, he lied to the Security Council. He says he was misled, and maybe he was misled. But I would have thought he would have known better. He showed us photographs of these trucks up in the north of Iraq, which he claimed were making biological weapons, and he must have recognized that they were, in fact, something else. I believe they were handling weather balloons. It was just an extraordinary display of dishonesty. And it must be a huge humiliation and embarrassment to him today, when he's out of power. I think the world recognizes he lied. And to lie to the Security Council and to encourage the aggression that took place, that's got to be classified as a war crime.

Washington has been systematically attacking the United Nations' Oil-for-Food programme that you were associated with. What's behind that?

Washington is under such pressure itself and so much criticism for the war and the failure of the occupation and the unending fighting and killing that's going on in Iraq that they're looking for something to divert attention away from themselves. Plus, you've got the age-old antagonism towards the United Nations in Washington. It goes back many, many years. And therefore, it was a glorious opportunity to attack the Secretary General in person and attack the organization.

There is an element of truth to it and, of course, that makes it interesting. The Secretary General's response of appointing the Volcker Commission was very clever. That's what he did to Rwanda and Srebrenica: look at yourself and announce *'mea culpa'*. But, in fact, we now have five or six investigations ongoing in Washington. I went voluntarily to Washington to brief a Senate committee and a committee of the House, to give them the information I thought they should have, because the withholding of information by Kofi Annan and Volcker I think is a huge mistake. It implies the Secretary is in fact guilty of something, and I don't believe that is the case.

The real scandal of the sanctions is taking Oil-for-Food revenue and giving 30% of it to Kuwait, while Iraqi children were dying for lack of decent water. The other scandal is to have a Washington that prosecutes Voices in the Wilderness for sending teddy bears to Iraqi kids but is allowing Saddam Hussein to sell oil to Turkey and to Jordan and have revenue in hard currency of approximately $10 billion. Those are the real scandals. The fact that one staff member may have walked away with $150,000 is appalling. I'm deeply shocked. But beside $10 billion, I think we have to put things in perspective.

Voices in the Wilderness, the Chicago-based human rights organization led by Kathy Kelly, is now called Voices for Creative Nonviolence. Explain the 30% going to Kuwait.

The moment the Oil-for-Food programme began, in 1996-97, and the revenue from oil sales went to the coffers of the United Nations, we, the United Nations Security Council, creamed off 30% from the gross, gave it to the United Nations Compensation Commission in Geneva, and they began a process of paying out compensation to private individuals, to companies, and to countries who had lost property, valuables, or whatever in Kuwait. Damage due to the Iraqi invasion. I'm not against compensation. You could wonder why Israel doesn't pay compensation to Lebanon, for example. But apart from that, when you have a country under sanctions and you have children dying by the thousand per month, to take money out of Iraqi hands, which could have been used to save lives, to pay a Cadillac salesman in Kuwait, that at best could have been postponed.

You say that the United Nations has been conspicuous in its collaboration with the so-called great powers, the United States and the United Kingdom, vis-à-vis Iraq.

In the days of the Coalition Provisional Authority and Mr. Bremer, our own man who represented the Secretary General worked cheek by jowl with the United States representative and was seen to be so doing. The United Nations was back in town despite the fact that an illegal invasion had taken place, an illegal occupation had been implemented, crimes had been committed and were being committed. And yet the UN was in there working with this foreign occupying force to begin to make changes in a country that had no representation, no legal government, I suppose, anymore. It's completely unacceptable. It's completely in breach of the way the United Nations does business with individual nation states. We work on the basis of invitation. We still respect sovereignty, right or wrong. We used different standards for Iraq, and we paid a very heavy price. The truck-bombing of the UN headquarters in Iraq should not take us by surprise, believe me. After sanctions and very open collaboration with the American armed forces, I think we should have anticipated something like that.

The Security Council refuses to define terrorism. Why is that?

I'm convinced — and this was part of the proposals of Kofi Annan for reform —

that terrorism needs to be acknowledged and recognized and defined. They have decided they can't do that because, I believe, they're afraid that they will see the issue of state terrorism addressed. And that will constrain their own ambitions for using terrorism as a device, as they do, such as the bombing of civilian areas or the use of depleted uranium or methods like 'Shock and Awe', which is designed to terrify a civilian population. This is unacceptable under international law, and they don't want to be constrained. Therefore, let's not worry about it. We just call resistance people the terrorists, and the rest of us are good guys. I think it's not really complicated.

The United States and, to a lesser extent, the United Kingdom have also been accused of blatant violations of the Geneva Conventions. What mechanism exists to impeach or prosecute states that are in violation of the Geneva Conventions? Will the United Nations do anything about it?

The way the Organization was created under the Charter, particularly in regard to the Security Council, and particularly in regard to the five permanent members, there is no provision for suspending those member states. They control that Organization. And if you look at the Charter and you want to change the Charter and reform the Organization, veto power remains in the hands of those five. If they don't like the reform proposals, they can veto it. So we have an impossible situation here. Nobody is going to attempt to punish the United States for breaking international law, breaking the Charter itself; there is no capacity to do that. And the other four permanent member states don't have the courage, because they're guilty themselves. Can the Russians really point at the Americans going into Afghanistan, when they've gone into Chechnya, for example, and committed atrocities?

And Afghanistan itself.

Indeed. They're all in bed together. And we're stuck with that scenario. And that's why very dramatic reform is required.

The General Assembly has not condemned the United States' invasion of Afghanistan or Iraq. Why not?

There were attempts to bring this to the General Assembly under the provision called Uniting for Peace. The precedent was set in the Korean War, when the Russians refused to endorse the Korean War in the Council. It was taken to the General Assembly and the majority, 66%, I believe, approved. There was an attempt to do that on the Iraq situation and prevent Mr. Bush from going to war by a vote in the General Assembly. The United States acted very quickly and bought off enough members of the General Assembly to avoid that sort of a vote. And I say 'buy off'. I'm talking about aid programmes and very practical measures of the World Bank and International Monetary Fund assistance. The United States controls these entities. It's not widely known, but the only veto power in the International Monetary Fund is that of the United States. So everybody needs Washington when it comes to the nitty-gritty of surviving as a nation state. Voting for or against Iraq becomes secondary.

As I look around us, the thought comes to mind that we are sitting here amidst the semi-ruins of a former empire – there is a kind of irony that we are talking about a current empire which sees itself as invincible. But all things will come to an end.

It's wonderful to be sitting here amidst the remains of the Ottoman Empire. But there are more and more Americans who are beginning to understand that empires all collapse and come to an end. I think many Americans, even if they're thinking only domestically, are concerned that something is falling apart here. And when they look at foreign policy, I think they understand that never has the United States, I think, been so isolated as it is at the moment, never has your country's foreign policy been so detested as it is at the moment.

You're setting up conflicts when the United States should be setting up relationships. You're not using the soft power that the United States has, or used to have, but instead using forms of aggression and pre-emptive aggression, which is frightening, terrifying for the rest of us — even those of us in Europe who perhaps no longer feel secure in the sense that we also might someday be invaded by the United States. We are still occupied to a certain extent, given American troops in Europe. But it has raised a level of anxiety which is very bad for the United States and will bring down this empire. The days are numbered. The American empire has peaked already. We're beginning to see a change, which I think will be in the best interests of all of us, including the people of the United States.

Turkey is a close Nato ally of the United States and has long been responsive to US demands. But on the issue of Iraq, Turkey decided actually to listen to its population, which was reporting astonishing figures, over 90%, in opposition to any Turkish military participation in the invasion of Iraq.

Very interesting. In Europe we sort of question Turkish democracy, but when it came to that issue, democracy worked very well here in Turkey. It did not work in Spain or Italy or Australia. Even in my own little country, the Irish government has allowed American war planes to land at Shannon Airport: armed troops on Irish soil, which is abhorrent to the Irish people. We've had enough of occupation under the British. So it was dramatic to see what the Turks managed to do. I can only take my hat off to Turkey in making the right decision.

This is the final session of the World Tribunal on Iraq. There has been a series of meetings in major cities around the world. What can be a positive outcome to these deliberations, considering the fact that the tribunal has no state authority or enforcement mechanisms to enforce its verdict?

Arundhati Roy called the Tribunal a resistance movement. The Tribunal represents resistance — resistance to what's happened in the United Nations, in the world today under this new era of pre-emptive aggression, which is so dangerous, this so-called humanitarian intervention, which has a different face in reality, sad to say. And I think the power that this Tribunal should have and maybe will have is the power of public opinion.

And perhaps it's a growing phenomenon. The peace and justice movement in the United States is a growing phenomenon. More and more Americans, disillusioned with Washington, are beginning to see some other side of the story and will act accordingly. This tribunal is just one part of a bigger picture, I think, of regular, ordinary people coming together, as they did on 15 February 2003, and demonstrating that this is not the way we want to see the world go. Aggression is not acceptable. We talk about ourselves being civilized. Let's behave in a civilized manner. And for a so-called American democracy led by this Christian born-again leader, to have a capability of going out and allowing 100,000 Iraqi civilians to be slaughtered, it's incomprehensible to me how he can reconcile his Christian caring together with his neglect of the well-being of the Iraqis, not forgetting American boys and girls who are going out there, again misinformed, believing they're fighting for the good old United States of America. In fact, they're throwing away their lives for a cause which has no validity.

Some suggestions?

It would be very good if the American school system began the introduction of human rights, looking at the Declaration of Human Rights. They need to understand what human rights mean for themselves and for other people; and that the United Nations is not an enemy, it's their friend. International law is also there to serve the people of the United States and protect their needs as it protects the little countries around the world. I think we're beginning to see in Washington that bright people are beginning to articulate that, indeed, respect for international law serves the interest of the United States. We've got to see a different attitude. We've got to have Americans look outwards, not only look inwards, and see that they are part of something bigger and that they need to participate in the United Nations and not just manipulate the UN in the vested interests of the United States itself.

Europe and Extraordinary Rendition

Tony Bunyan

Tony Bunyan is the Director of Statewatch, the civil liberties and human rights organization. He is also a regular participant in the conferences of the European Network for Peace and Human Rights (see Spokesman 86). In January 2006, he was invited to address Members of the European Parliament on the United States' use of European countries for the illegal transportation and detention of prisoners in the process known as 'extraordinary rendition' (see Spokesman 89). This article is based on his speech.

What do we know? Some examples are that in Spain 42 suspected Central Intelligence Agency operatives are sought – at least 18 of whom have addresses near Langley, the CIA headquarters. Their names were traced through luxury hotels in Palma and Mallorca.

A fax intercepted by Swiss secret services from the Egyptian Foreign Ministry to their embassy in London said that 23 Iraqi and Afghan prisoners were interrogated at a Romanian military base on the Black Sea.

Alvaro Gil-Robles (Council of Europe Human Rights Commissioner) says that there is a camp at US base 'Bondsteel' outside Priština (in Kosovo) that looks like Guantánamo Bay.

One of the first cases of extraordinary rendition we know took place in Sweden on 18 December 2001. Muhammed Al Zery and Ahmed Agiza from Egypt were granted asylum in 1999 and 2000 respectively. They were arrested by Swedish Security Police and taken to Bromma airport were the executive jet N379P had landed. They were handed over to hooded CIA agents who cut the clothes from their bodies, sedated them, dressed them in overalls, chained their hands and feet, and flown to Egypt, where they were tortured.

A case study from the United Kingdom*

The first of the overall issues I want to look at is the role of European Union governments who have turned a 'blind eye' to rendition flights. I want to do this by examining the position of the United Kingdom.

On 10 February 2005, *The Independent* newspaper published a story saying that two executive jets were using British airports to carry out CIA renditions. (*The Independent on Sunday*, 20 February 2005, developed the story.)

On 25 February 2005, the House of

---

* Sources primarily *Hansard*, the official Parliamentary record.

Commons Select Committee on Foreign Affairs wrote to the Foreign Secretary asking whether the UK government allowed any other country 'to use its territory or its airspace [for renditions]'. On 12 September 2005, the allegations were pinned down when *The Guardian* newspaper detailed 210 CIA flights into the United Kingdom – the data had been gathered in the United States.

The Central Intelligence Agency had used 19 British airports and Royal Air Force bases including Heathrow, Gatwick, Birmingham, Luton, Bournemouth and Belfast, plus 75 flights through Prestwick in Scotland, 74 through Glasgow, and 33 through RAF Northolt (near London).

There was now substantial concern about the 210 recorded flights (later to rise to 400). There was also concern at the use of United Kingdom airspace. For example, CIA planes using Shannon airport on the west coast of Ireland (recorded 43 times) would most likely use United Kingdom airspace to or from their destinations.

In October 2005, the Foreign and Commonwealth Office issued a statement saying:

> 'The government are not aware of the use of their territory or airspace for the purposes of extraordinary rendition. The government have not received any request nor granted any permissions for the use of UK territory or airspace for such purposes'.

On 16 November 2005, the Ministry of Defence and Foreign and Commonwealth Office said it:

> 'has not authorised, nor received any requests for the use of UK airspace or airports for those involuntarily transferred'.

On 17 November 2005, in a written answer, the Ministry of Defence said it maintained records of all civil registered planes landing at UK military airfields. The record included the plane's registration number, name of the pilot, departure date and destination. It was, said the answer, not required to have the names of the passengers.

What about the use of RAF Northolt 33 times?

On 12 December 2005, the Department of Transport set out the legal position under the Chicago Convention on Civil Aviation 1944 (the UK Civil Aviation Act 1982). Under Article 9 a state may restrict or prohibit aircraft flying over its territory on a number of grounds including 'public safety', i.e. the safety and well-being of any passengers. Scheduled flights need permission, which can be denied. Non-scheduled flights need permission including 'where payment is made for carriage' – it is unclear what this term means, but could it include payment for refuelling? All other aircraft have the right to land or fly across the United Kingdom without prior permission. However, each captain has to file a flight plan with Eurocontrol, the European Organisation for the Safety of Air Navigation*.

---

*The practice whereby civil aircraft using military or civilian airfields do not have to give the names of the passengers, or where planes can similarly overfly a country, seems an extraordinary breach in security arrangements. For example, under the Police and Criminal Justice Bill currently going through Parliament the details of all passengers on internal UK flights have to be registered and checked.

On the same day, 12 December 2005, Jack Straw, the Foreign Secretary, replied to a question:

'We would not assist ... where there were grounds to believe that the person would face a real risk of torture'

Why does the Foreign Secretary refer only to 'torture' and not to inhuman and degrading treatment, as well? He went on to say to say that there had been 'No requests since 11 September 2001'.

There had been two cases in 1998, when the United Kingdom had agreed, to enable people to stand trial in the United States. There had also been a request in 1998 for the transfer of a person to a third country, which he thought had been refused.

Throughout this period, innumerable questions about the role of British intelligence or security agencies (MI6 and MI5) were met with the standard answer: 'It is not the Government's policy to comment on intelligence matters'. However, in January 2006 there was a very significant shift in the government's response. On 23 January, a letter from the Foreign Secretary to Sir Menzies Campbell (Liberal Democrat spokesperson) finally gave the game away. Mr Straw said that as part of close cooperation in fighting terrorism with the United States the government had now:

'made clear to the US authorities [that]...
i) we expect them to seek permission to render detainees via United Kingdom territory and airspace
ii) permission would only be granted if they were satisfied the rendition would accord with United Kingdom law and our international obligations.'

The third point referred to the United Kingdom's understanding of obligations under the UN Convention on Torture, as distinct from the US interpretation, which sought not only to limit obligations about torture, but also sought to narrow the interpretation of what torture means. It thus refers to any 'rendition', not just 'extraordinary rendition'.

The government had, finally, been forced publicly to set out a new policy.

On the very same day, 23 January, the *New Statesman* magazine published an article by Martin Bright revealing the content of a leaked memorandum from the Senior Legal Advisor in the Foreign Office to the Prime Minister's Office. The memo said that extraordinary rendition was 'almost certainly illegal'. That rendition – the transfer of a person from one jurisdiction to another – might be legal but in very, very limited circumstances as the International Covenant on Civil and Political Rights and the European Convention on Human Rights imposed obligations where 'a person is arbitrarily detained or expelled outside the normal legal process'. Furthermore, though the United States says it relies on 'assurances' that people will not be tortured, 'we should not cast doubt as we are doing the same things, e.g. Algeria, etc.'*

---

* The United Kingdom has sought 'assurances' against torture and execution from Jordan, Libya, Algeria and Morocco, in order to deport people to these countries since they have insufficient evidence to bring them to court in the UK.

On a related issue, the memo asks:

> Question: 'How do we know whether those our Armed Forces helped to capture in Iraq or Afghanistan have subsequently been sent to interrogation centres?'
> Answer: 'We have no mechanism for establishing this'.

In other words they do not know, and do not care. This sums up the attitude of the United Kingdom government (and other European Union governments) towards CIA flights and rendition. Having talked to those in touch with intelligence sources, their attitude, reflecting government policy, was summed up by one source: 'We turned a blind eye, we don't want to know.'

The role of European Union intelligence agencies

The second issue I want to address is the role of European Union agencies (intelligence and security) in targeting suspects, putting them under surveillance, and sharing intelligence between themselves and with the United States. In other words, what part have European Union intelligence and security agencies played in targeting people, whether in the European Union or outside?

In the United Kingdom we know that, as long ago as June 1976, at the inception of the Trevi group, in the fight against terrorism MI5 was designated as the contact point for 'intelligence', while 'policing matters' went to the police. MI5 has thus had, for a very long time, a remit alongside MI6 (the Secret Intelligence Service or SIS, external) within the European Union.

In July 2005, MI6 supplied the Greek authorities with a list of 5,364 people to be investigated in the wake of the 7 and 21 July attacks in London. Such a list would likely have been drawn up jointly by MI5 and MI6. As a result 1,212 people were arrested and interrogated. And, in a separate intelligence operation, 28 Pakistani men were abducted and held for between two and six days, with MI6 officers in attendance (see *Spokesman 89*). How many other European Union states were sent lists?

I was alerted, in November 2005, to a *Der Speigel* article on 'Camolin' (sometimes referred to as 'Alliance Base'). This is an intelligence operation involving agencies from the United States, Germany, France, United Kingdom, Canada and Australia. It is based at a military barracks outside Paris where regular meetings take place – backed by a secure communications network.

Apparently the *modus operandi* is that European Union intelligence agencies build up dossiers on suspected individuals (in Iraq, Afghanistan, etc) which are handed over to the CIA to act on – rendition, detention, interrogation, assassination? Who knows? 'Camolin' may be just one example of a hidden network of CIA-funded centres called Counter Terrorist Intelligence Centres. In the spring of 2005, the CIA's Deputy Director of Operations, Jose A Rodriguez Jnr, told a closed session of the House and Senate Intelligence Committee that more than 25 Counter Terrorist Intelligence Centres were responsible for over 3,000 arrests. The list of countries with such Centres is said to include sixteen in Europe, six in Asia, eight in the Middle East/North Africa, plus Australia and

Canada. If there are sixteen in Europe, including ones in France, Italy, Germany, Poland and Romania, what are they doing?

Apparently, the Centres' *modus operandi* varies from country to country – from those countries with whom the CIA works closely, which have trusted agencies, to those where the national agencies are not trusted or corrupt. In the latter case, the CIA hires experts or specific local units (with the tacit approval of governments).

The question of transit for CIA flights

There have been informal agreements between European Union governments and the United States to allow stop-over flights (in transit) to and from the United States since around 1998. This was to send people (refugees) back to Africa, the Middle East and Asia.

A year after the invasion of Iraq, there was the 'New Transatlantic Agenda: EU-US meeting on Justice and Home Affairs' in Athens. The minutes record that 'Both sides agreed on ... increased use of European transit facilities to support the return of criminals and inadmissible aliens'. Who are the 'criminals'? Are they convicted or suspected, and of what crimes? Who are the 'inadmissible aliens'? Why, and where are they being returned to? In addition to the why and the where and the future they might face, there is the crucial question: under what conditions are these people being transited in and through the European Union? Are they shackled or sedated?

No figures have ever been published of how many flights there have been – whether for criminals, refugees or those being rendered. A number of European Union governments have colluded, simply by turning a 'blind eye', failing to ask any questions. So that, if asked, they could say no requests for transit or over-flying have been received.

All European Union governments should be required to tell the United States that:

a. they have to seek permission to render detainees (whether as part of the 'war on terrorism', as criminals or refugees) via their territory or airspace.
b. that permission would only be granted if they are satisfied that national and international obligations are being met, including those on torture, inhuman or degrading treatment.
c. to this end, all non-scheduled flights would be required to provide the names of all passengers – in addition to that information already required – and to say whether any of the passengers are restrained or sedated in any way.
d. that assurances from the United States as to meeting these obligations would be subject to random spot checks at any point of transit in the European Union.

If the United States has nothing to hide, then it has nothing to fear.

Drawn To That Moment

John Berger

John Berger, writer and critic, is the author of The Success and Failure of Picasso *and* Art and Revolution *among many other works. First published in 1976, this essay forms part of* Berger on Drawing, *a beautiful volume published by the Occasional Press in Cork on 2005. We are very grateful to the author for permission to reprint it, and we thank David Lilburn and Jim Savage who 'are the Occasional Press'.*

When my father died recently, I did several drawings of him in his coffin. Drawings of his face and head. There is a story about Kokoschka teaching a life class. The students were uninspired. So he spoke to the model and instructed him to pretend to collapse. When he had fallen over, Kokoschka rushed over to him, listened to his heart and announced to the shocked students that he was dead. A little afterwards the model got to his feet and resumed the pose. 'Now draw him,' said Kokoschka, 'as though you were aware that he was alive and not dead.'

One can imagine that the students, after this theatrical experience, drew with more verve. Yet to draw the truly dead involves an ever-greater sense of urgency. What you are drawing will never be seen again, by you or by anybody else. In the whole course of time past and time to come, this moment is unique: the last opportunity to draw what will never again be visible, which has occurred once and will never reoccur. Because the faculty of sight is continuous, because visual categories (red, yellow, dark, thick, thin) remain constant, and because so many things appear to remain in place, one tends to forget that the visual is always a result of an unrepeatable, momentary encounter. Appearances, at any given moment, are a construction emerging from the debris of everything that has previously appeared. It is something like this that I understand in those words of Cézanne, which so often come back to me: 'One minute in the life of the world is going by. Paint it as it is.'

Beside my father's coffin I summoned such skill as I have as a draughtsman to apply it *directly* to the task in hand. I say directly because often skill in drawing expresses itself as a manner, and then its application to what is being drawn is indirect.

Mannerism – in the general rather than art-historical sense – comes from the need to invent urgency, to produce an 'urgent' drawing, instead of submitting to the urgency of what is. Here I was using my small skill to save a likeness, as a lifesaver uses his much greater skill as a swimmer to save a life. People talk of freshness of vision, of the intensity of seeing for the first time, but the intensity of seeing for the last time is, I believe, greater. Of all that I could see only the drawing would remain. I wept whilst I strove to draw with complete objectivity.

As I drew his mouth, his brows, his eyelids, as their specific forms emerged with lines from the whiteness of the paper, I felt the history and the experience which had made them as they were. His life was now as finite as the rectangle of paper on which I was drawing, but within it, in a way infinitely more mysterious than any drawing, his character and destiny had emerged. I was making a record and his face was already only a record of his life. Each drawing then was nothing but the site of a departure.

They remained. I looked at them and found that they resembled my father. Or, more strictly, that they resembled him as he was when dead. Nobody could ever mistake these drawings as ones of an old man sleeping. Why not? I ask myself. And the answer, I think, is in the way they are drawn. Nobody could draw a sleeping man with such objectivity. About this quality there is finality. Objectivity is what is left when something is finished.

I chose one drawing to frame and hang on the wall in front of the table at which I work. Gradually and consistently the relationship of my father to his drawing changed – or changed for me.

There are several ways of describing the change. The content of the drawing increased. The drawing, instead of marking the site of departure, began to mark the site of an arrival. The forms, drawn, filled out. The drawing became the immediate locus of my memories of my father. The drawing was, no longer deserted but inhabited. For each form, between the pencil marks and the white paper they marked, there was now a door through which moments of a life could enter: the drawing, instead of being simply an object of perception with one face, had moved forward to become double-faced, and worked like a filter, from behind, it drew out my memories of the past whilst, forwards, it projected an image which, unchanging, was becoming increasingly familiar. My father came back to give the image of his death mask a kind of life. If I look at the drawing now, I scarcely see the face of a dead man; instead I see aspects of my father's life. Yet if somebody from the village came in, he would see only a drawing of a death mask. It is still unmistakably that. The change which has taken place is subjective. Yet, in a more general sense, if such a subjective process did not exist, neither would drawings.

The advent of the cinema and television means that we now define drawings (or paintings) as static images. What we often overlook it that their virtue, their very function, depended upon this. The need to discover the camera, and the instantaneous or moving image, arose for many different reasons but it was not in order to improve on the static image, or, if it was presented in those terms, it was only because the meaning of the static image had been lost. In the nineteenth century when social time became unilinear, vectorial and regularly exchangeable, the instant became the maximum which could be grasped or preserved. The plate camera and the pocket watch, the reflex camera and the wrist-watch, are twin inventions. A drawing or painting presupposes another view of time.

Any image – like the image read from the retina – records an appearance which will disappear. The faculty of sight developed as an active response to continually changing contingencies. The more it developed, the more complex the view of appearances it could construct from events. (An event in itself has no appearances.) Recognition is an essential part of this construction. And recognition depends upon the phenomenon of reappearance sometimes occurring in the ceaseless flux of disappearance. Thus, if appearances, at any given moment, are a construction emerging from the debris of all that has previously appeared, it is understandable that this very construction may give birth to the idea that everything will one day be recognizable, and the flux of disappearance cease. Such an idea is more than a personal dream; it has supplied the energy for a large part of human culture. For example: the story triumphs over oblivion; music offers a centre; the drawing challenges disappearance.

What is the nature of this challenge? A fossil also 'challenges' disappearance but the challenge is meaningless. A photograph challenges disappearance but its challenge is different from that of the fossil or the drawing.

The fossil is the result of random chance. The photographed image has been selected for preservation. The drawn image contains the experience of looking. A photographer is evidence of an encounter between event and photographer. A drawing slowly questions an event's appearance and in so doing reminds us that appearances are always a construction with a history. (Our aspiration towards objectivity can only proceed from the admission of subjectivity.) We use photographs by taking them with us, in our lives, our arguments, our memories; it is we who move them. Whereas a drawing or painting forces us to stop and enter its time. A photograph is static because it has stopped time. A drawing or painting is static because it encompasses time.

I should perhaps explain here why I make a certain distinction between drawings and paintings. Drawings reveal the process of their own making, their own looking, more clearly. The imitative facility of a painting often acts as a disguise – i.e. what it refers to becomes more impressive than the reason for referring to it. Great paintings are not disguised in this way. But even a third-rate drawing reveals the process of its own creation.

How does a drawing or painting encompass time? What does it hold in its stillness? A drawing is more than a momento – a device for bringing back memories of the time past. The 'space' that my drawing offers for my father's return into it is quite distinct from that offered by a letter from him, an object owned by him or, as I have tried to explain, a photograph of him. And here it is incidental that I am looking at a drawing which I drew myself. An equivalent drawing by anybody else would offer the same 'space'.

To draw is to look, to examine the spectrum of appearance. A drawing of a tree shows, not a tree, but a tree being-looked-at. Whereas the sight of a tree is registered almost instantaneously, the examination of the sight of a tree (a tree being-looked-at) not only takes minutes or hours instead of a fraction of a second, it also involves, derives from, and refers back to, much previous experience of looking. Within the instant of the sight of a tree is established a life-experience. This is how the act of drawing refuses the process of disappearances and proposes the simultaneity of a multitude of moments.

From each glance a drawing assembles a little evidence, but it consists of the evidence of many glances which can be seen together. On the one hand there is no sight in nature as unchanging as that of a drawing or a painting. On the other hand, what is unchanging in a drawing consists of so many assembled moments that they constitute a totality rather than a fragment. The static image of a drawing or painting is the result of the opposition of two dynamic processes. Disappearances opposed by assemblage. If, for diagrammatic convenience, one accepts the metaphor of time as a flow, a river, then the act of drawing, by driving upstream, achieves the stationary.

Vermeer's view of Delft across the canal explains this as no theoretical explanation can ever. The painted moment has remained (almost) unchanged for three centuries. The reflections in the water have not moved. Yet this painted moment, as we look at it, has a plenitude of actuality that we experience only rarely in life. We experience everything we see in the painting as *absolutely* momentary. At the same time the experience is repeatable the next day or in ten years. It would be naïve to suppose that this has to do with accuracy: Delft at any given moment never looked like this painting. It has to do with the density per square millimetre of Vermeer's looking, with the density per square millimetre of assembled moments.

As a drawing, the drawing above my table is unremarkable. But it works in accord with the same hopes and principles which have led men to draw for thousands of years. It works because from being a site of departure, it has become a site of arrival.

Every day more of my father's life returns to the drawing in front of me.

Drawn To That Moment first appeared in *New Society* magazine, 1976. Published in *The White Bird* by Hogarth Press, 1985.

THE BERTRAND RUSSELL PEACE FOUNDATION
DOSSIER

2006   Number 19

BEYOND ABU GHRAIB

Some 14,000 people are currently imprisoned in Iraq by the United States and United Kingdom military, according to official figures. The circumstances of the detention of these people are examined in Amnesty International's report 'Beyond Abu Ghraib: Detention and Torture in Iraq', from which these excerpts are taken. It was published in March 2006.

... Since the invasion of Iraq in March 2003 tens of thousands of people have been detained by foreign forces, mainly the United States forces, without being charged or tried and without the right to challenge their detention before a judicial body. Between August 2004 and November 2005 an administrative review board (the Combined Review and Release Board), composed of representatives of the Multinational Force and the Iraqi government, examined the files of almost 22,000 internees and recommended about 12,000 for release and another 10,000 for continued detention. The vast majority of 'security internees' – that is those individuals held in connection with the on-going armed conflict who are considered by the Multinational Force to be a threat to security – have never been tried. According to statistical data compiled by the Multinational Force, by the end of November 2005, the Central Criminal Court of Iraq had tried 1,301 alleged insurgents ...

Most 'security internees' are held at four detention facilities under United States control, namely Camp Bucca near Basra, Abu Ghraib prison in Baghdad, Camp Cropper in Baghdad and Fort Suse near Suleimaniya, which started operating at the end of October 2005. In addition, US forces hold detainees temporarily in various brigade and division internment facilities throughout the country. A small number of 'security internees' are held in the custody of United Kingdom forces at the detention facility of Shu'aiba Camp, near Basra. According to the United Kingdom's Foreign and Commonwealth Office, at the end of October 2005, the UK forces held 33 security internees, none of whom were women or children, in their detention facility at al-Shu'aiba.

At the beginning of 2004 the Coalition Provisional Authority headed by US ambassador Paul Bremer published a list of about 8,500 detainees on the Internet. However, the true figure of those then being held was believed to be much higher. When the Authority was disbanded in June 2004, the number of detainees held by the Coalition Forces had fallen to about 6,400 persons, according to a US military official. However, since the handover of power, the number of detainees held by the Multinational Force has increased steadily.

In November 2004, General Geoffrey Miller, then US head of Iraqi detainee operations, stated that about 8,300 detainees were held by the Multinational Force. On 1 April 2005, the US Department of State estimated the number of detainees at about 10,000 persons. According to the official website of the Multinational Force, at the end of November 2005 there were more than 14,000 security detainees held in Multinational Force custody, distributed over the four main US controlled detention centres as follows: Abu Ghraib prison (4,710 detainees), Camp Bucca (7,365 detainees), Camp Cropper (138 detainees) and Fort Suse (1,176 detainees), as well as various military brigade and division internment facilities (650 detainees).

Legal background to detentions by the Multinational Force

Following the US-led invasion in March 2003, Iraq was in a state of international armed conflict. Consequently, persons deprived of their liberty by the occupying forces were protected – in addition to applicable human rights law – by international humanitarian law, namely the Third (Convention relative to the Treatment of Prisoners of War) or the Fourth (Convention relative to the Protection of Civilian Persons in Time of War) Geneva Conventions of 1949. The deprivation of liberty of a person which is ordered by the executive power without bringing charges against that person is referred to as administrative detention or internment. The Fourth Geneva Convention, applicable in situations of international armed conflict, states that internment 'may be ordered only if the security of the Detaining Power makes it absolutely necessary'.

With the handover of power in June 2004 the legal situation changed; since then Iraq is considered to be in a situation of non-international armed conflict with the Multinational Force and the Iraqi security forces on one side and the insurgents on the other. Therefore, the Geneva Conventions no longer fully apply to persons detained in connection with the ongoing armed conflict. In this situation, all parties including the Multinational Force are bound by Article 3 common to the four Geneva Conventions, and by customary rules applicable to non-international armed conflicts, as well as human rights law. Article 3 common to the Four Geneva Conventions requires that those placed in detention are treated humanely, though it does not contain detailed provisions regulating such detention.

Since the handover of power, the Multinational Force refer to UN Security Council Resolution 1546 as providing the legal basis for the MNF forces to hold people in detention in Iraq. Resolution 1546, with its attached exchange of letters between, for the United States, Secretary of State Colin Powell and, for Iraq, Prime Minister Ayad Allawi, confers on the Multinational Force authority to resort to 'internment where this is necessary for imperative reasons of security'. Unfortunately, there is no reference in Resolution 1546 to the legal safeguards that are to apply to arrests, detention or internment carried out by armed forces and troops from countries contributing to the Multinational Force. The United Kingdom and the United States have stated, however, that their internment policies are also governed by Coalition Provisional Authority Memorandum No. 3 (revised) of June 2004, which sets out the process of arrest and detention of criminal suspects, as well as procedures relating to 'security internees' detained by members of the Multinational Force after 28 June 2004.

This Coalition Provisional Authority Memorandum, which was revised only one day before the handover of power, details the authority of the Multinational Force to detain people in Iraq. It elaborates some procedural details regarding detentions by the Multinational Force and distinguishes between 'criminal detainees' and 'security internees'. With regard to criminal detainees the document stipulates: '(…) the Multinational Force shall have the right to apprehend persons who are suspected of having committed criminal acts and are not considered security internees (hereafter: "criminal detainees") who shall be handed over to the Iraqi authorities as soon as reasonably practicable'.

The Memorandum established some basic rules for the detention of 'security internees', concerning review procedures, access to internees and other aspects of their conditions, and the maximum period of internment of children. Coalition Provisional Authority Memorandum No.3 provides that anyone who is interned for more than 72 hours is entitled to have the decision to intern them reviewed within seven days and thereafter at intervals of no more than six months. The Memorandum also states that the 'operation, condition and standards of any internment facility established by the Multinational Force shall be in accordance with Section IV of the Fourth Geneva Convention'.

Procedures set out in the Coalition Provisional Authority Memorandum and those which have been developed in practice are crucially flawed because they fail to meet international human rights standards guaranteeing the rights of detainees – including, notably, the right to have access to legal counsel and the right to challenge the lawfulness of the detention before a court.

In addition to the provisions of international humanitarian law related to non-international armed conflict set out above, human rights law remains applicable to Iraq. The United States, the United Kingdom and Iraq are all states parties to the International Covenant on Civil and Political Rights, which provides basic safeguards for the protection of detainees. As affirmed by the UN Human Rights Committee (the expert UN body responsible for overseeing the implementation of the Covenant), international humanitarian law and human rights law fully complement one another during times of armed conflict. The relevant treaties governing non-international armed conflict do not contain specific rules regarding questions such as for what duration and under what procedures (Protocol II explicitly accepts internment but does not regulate it) persons may be interned. It is human rights law that squarely addresses this question.

Amnesty International considers the Multinational Force system of security internment in Iraq to be arbitrary – in violation of fundamental human rights. All detainees, including security internees, are protected by Article 9 of the

Convention, which provides that no-one should be subjected to arbitrary detention and that deprivation of liberty must be based on grounds and procedures established by law (para 1). Detainees must also have access to a court empowered to rule without delay on the lawfulness of their detention and to order their release if the detention is found to be unlawful (para 4). These requirements apply to 'anyone who is deprived of his liberty by arrest or detention' and therefore apply fully to those interned by the Multinational Force.

The Convention (under Article 4) does allow for derogation of some provisions of the Covenant during proclaimed states of emergency, including at a time of armed conflict. However, measures derogating from the Covenant are allowed only if and to the extent that the situation constitutes a threat to the life of the nation. The Human Rights Committee has emphasized that 'States parties may in no circumstances invoke Article 4 of the Covenant as justification for acting in violation of humanitarian law or peremptory norms of international law, for instance ... through arbitrary deprivations of liberty'. Neither the United States nor the United Kingdom governments, however, have taken the steps necessary formally to derogate from any of their obligations under the Convention (which derogation requires that governments notify the Human Rights Committee formally of their intention to derogate from relevant Convention provisions).

At all times, internees must be provided the right to an effective remedy (Convention Article 3(2)), including *habeas corpus*, so that a court may decide without delay on the lawfulness of the detention and order release if the detention is not lawful (Article 9(4)). A person detained on suspicion of criminal activity must be brought promptly before a judge (Convention Article 9(3)) and either released or provided a fair trial before an independent and impartial tribunal established by law (Convention Article 14).

Review process

Jawad M, an Iraqi national who worked for the US forces at military bases in Baghdad, was detained by US forces in August 2004. In October 2004 he received a document from the Office of the Deputy Commanding General, Detainee Operations, Multinational Force-Iraq which informed him about an upcoming review session and included the following one-sentence accusation: 'Gathering of information on interpreters and employees with the Multinational Force'. No further explanation or reference to any relevant legislation was provided. He was not charged or tried. Reviews of his case were conducted by an administrative body before which he was not permitted to appear. Following his release from Abu Ghraib prison at the beginning of 2005, Jawad M told Amnesty International that he still did not know the reasons for his internment. He said: 'It was useless. I was there for five months and I knew that nobody can do anything. Until now I don't know why they sent me to the prison and why I was released and whose decision that was.'

The case of Jawad M illustrates the way in which many internees are detained arbitrarily by the Multinational Force. In violation of international human rights law, tens of thousands of internees have been held for weeks or months and thousands for more than one year without being charged or tried and with no right to challenge the lawfulness of their detention before a judicial body. They have received no information regarding the grounds for their detention, whether they will be charged and brought to trial or, if not, for how long they are likely to be detained.

As detailed below, the United States and United Kingdom have established separate systems for reviewing cases of internees held by their respective forces. Both systems have in common that they fail to meet international human rights law and standards – including the requirement for court oversight of the detention. Despite the involvement of consultative bodies in the process, the ultimate decision about the release or continued internment of a person lies with military commanders.

Review for internees held by US forces

The Multinational Force's internment procedures were criticised by Iraqi Justice Minister 'Abd al-Hussain Shandal in September 2005. Speaking to *Reuters* news agency, he complained: 'No citizen should be arrested without a court order (…) There is abuse [of human rights] due to detentions, which are overseen by the Multinational Force and are not in the control of the Justice Ministry'.

Since the handover of power in mid-2004, however, the Iraqi authorities have participated in reviewing cases of internees held by the Multinational Force in line with changes announced by the US Department of Defense in August 2004.

After the handover, a body called the Combined Review and Release Board was established, comprising two representatives each from the Iraqi ministries of Justice, the Interior and Human Rights and three Multinational Force officers. This body reviews the cases of internees and makes recommendations regarding their release or continued detention – according to Human Rights Ministry officials these recommendations are made by majority and none of the board's members has a power of veto – but its recommendations are not binding and it is the Multinational Force's Deputy Commanding General for Detainee Operations who decides whether or not a detainee should be released after first consulting Iraq's Minister of Justice.

The US government's 2005 report to the UN Committee against Torture provided the following description of the detention review process:

> 'Upon capture by a detaining unit, a detainee is moved as expeditiously as possible to a theater internment facility. A military magistrate reviews an individual's detention to assess whether to continue to detain or to release him or her. If detention is continued, the Combined Review and Release Board assumes the responsibility for subsequently reviewing whether continued detention is appropriate.'

Coalition Provisional Authority Memorandum No. 3 stipulates that the review within seven days must be followed by further reviews at intervals of no more than six months. In practice, these appear generally to be respected with some reviews being done at more frequent intervals. In considering cases, the Combined Review and Release Board has three possible options to recommend: unconditional release, release with a suitable guarantor from the detainee's community, or continued internment. Neither the internee nor his or her legal counsel are permitted to be present during these case reviews, though internees have reportedly been encouraged to make submissions to the Combined Review and Release Board in writing.

Between the establishment of the Combined Review and Release Board in August 2004 and 28 November 2005, the Board reviewed the files of 21,995 internees, of whom 4,426 were recommended for unconditional release, 7,626 for release with a guarantor and 9,903 for continued internment. According to the US Department of Defense, the Combined Review and Release Board when making a decision is to take into consideration the 'circumstances of the detainee's capture, the length of detention prior to review, the level of cooperation by the detainee, and the detainee's potential for further acts of anti-Iraqi misconduct if released'.

In its report to the UN Committee against Torture, the US government referred to the practice of having a military magistrate conduct the initial review within seven days, but such reviews appear generally to be paper-based reviews, in which the internee's file is considered without his being present.

In one case that received considerable media attention, however, a security internee was permitted to be present during the review of his detention conducted by US military officers. But the review procedure followed in the case of 44-year-old US national **Cyrus Kar**, a film-maker, differed from the normal procedure. Kar and his cameraman, **Farshid Faraji**, were detained on 17 May 2005 by Iraqi security forces while riding a taxi in Baghdad. Whilst Farshid Faraji was held for almost two months in detention by the Iraqi authorities, Cyrus Kar was handed over to the US forces. Kar was denied access to a lawyer during his detention but on 4 July 2005 he was brought before a review board composed of three US military officers. He was released on 10 July, after which he commented: 'I couldn't have more respect for the rank-and-file soldiers, but the system is broken. When an Iraqi is detained there, he comes out angry and wanting payback'.

Review for internees held by UK forces

Cases of detainees interned by United Kingdom forces are reviewed by the Divisional Internment Review Committee, which is composed entirely of Multinational Force officials. Its members are the United Kingdom military chief of staff, another senior officer, the chief legal officer and another legal officer and the chief political advisor. However, the final decision as to whether a detainee should continue to be interned or released rests with the Governing Officer Commanding.

The initial review has to take place within 48 hours of internment and thereafter monthly. An interned person may address written submissions to the Divisional Internment Review Committee, but neither the internee nor his or her legal representative may be present when the Committee reviews the internee's case.

The Governing Officer Commanding informs internees in writing, stating the reasons, when it is determined that they should continue to be interned. However, Amnesty International is concerned that even after months of internment the Multinational Force continues to hold internees without providing them or their legal counsel with substantive evidence to justify their detention.

For example, a 48-year-old dual national with UK and Iraqi citizenship, **Hillal 'Abdul Razzaq 'Ali al-Jedda,** has been detained since his arrest on 10 October 2004 in Baghdad. He filed a case against the United Kingdom Secretary of State for Defence challenging his internment in Iraq, which was dismissed by the High Court of England and Wales on 12 August 2005. However, the court noted that 'Although detained for imperative reasons of security, the claimant has not been charged with any offence; and the Secretary of State acknowledges that, as matters stand, there is insufficient material available which could be used in court to support criminal charges against him. The claimant is therefore detained simply on a preventive basis.' In mid-February 2006, Hillal 'Abdul Razzaq 'Ali al-Jedda continued to be held without charge or trial by United Kingdom forces. In January 2006, an appeal against the decision of the High Court was heard in the Court of Appeal of England and Wales but judgment was still awaited in mid-February.

Length of internment

Different provisions exist for detainees held by the Multinational Force since before the mid-2004 transfer of power to a new Iraqi government and those detained since that time. Detainees in the first category may be held indefinitely, whereas those detained and interned since 30 June 2004, according to Coalition Provisional Authority Memorandum No. 3, 'must be either released from internment or transferred to the Iraqi criminal jurisdiction no later than 18 months from the date of induction into a Multinational Force internment facility.'

This requirement of release after 18 months is not absolute, however. Even the detainees interned after the handover can be held for more prolonged periods at the approval of the Joint Detention Committee. This requires that an application for further internment is made to the Joint Detention Committee two months before the expiry of the initial internment period of 18 months; if the Committee sanctions continued internment it must specify the duration. According to the Human Rights Annual Report 2005 of the United Kingdom Foreign and Commonwealth Office, published in July 2005, the Joint Detention Committee had still to be convened for UK-held internees because none of them by then had been held for as long as 18 months. In mid-February 2006 an application for the extension of internment beyond 18 months of 266 detainees had been made to the Joint Detention Committee.

Amnesty International is concerned about hundreds of security internees who have been detained by the Multinational Force since before the handover of power and may be held indefinitely. In a letter to Amnesty International dated 19 February 2006, Major General Gardner, commander of Task Force 134, which is in charge of Multinational Force detention operations, stated that at the end of

2005 the number of security internees held for more than 18 months was estimated to be 751. The letter confirmed that approval by the Joint Detention Committee to keep an internee beyond 18 months is only required for 'internees detained after 30 June 2004'.

Amnesty International considers indefinite internment as practised by the Multinational Force with regard to security internees held since before the handover of power to be unlawful. According to The UN Working Group on Arbitrary Detentions (established by the UN Commission on Human Rights):

> 'With regard to derogations that are unlawful and inconsistent with States' obligations under international law, the Working Group reaffirms that the fight against terrorism may undeniably require specific limits on certain guarantees, including those concerning detention and the right to a fair trial. It nevertheless points out that under any circumstances, and whatever the threat, there are rights which cannot be derogated from, that *in no event may an arrest based on emergency legislation last indefinitely*, and it is particularly important that measures adopted in states of emergency should be strictly commensurate with the extent of the danger invoked.'

Amnesty International also considers that indefinite internment may constitute a violation of the prohibition on torture and other cruel, inhuman or degrading treatment or punishment. Any deprivation of liberty, even when carried out in accordance with international humanitarian law, inevitably causes some stress or a degree of mental suffering to the internee and his or her family, although this will not automatically render the deprivation unlawful. However, Amnesty International is concerned that the 'security internees' held by the Multinational Force, are being deprived of their liberty in circumstances that cause unnecessary suffering, such as indefinite and incommunicado detention, that cannot be justified as an unavoidable part of a 'lawful sanction'. The UN Committee against Torture has found that administrative detention by a party to an armed conflict may constitute cruel, inhuman or degrading treatment or punishment, based *inter alia* on its excessive length. In addition, the Human Rights Committee has referred to prolonged, indefinite 'administrative detention' as incompatible with Article 7 of the International Convention on Civil and Political Rights, which prohibits, among other things, torture and cruel, inhuman or degrading treatment or punishment.

Indefinite detention causes uncertainty and mental anguish for many internees in Iraq – some of whom have been held for more than two years. Many relatives of detainees with whom Amnesty International has been in regular contact have expressed their despair. For example, in January 2006 the organization received the following email communication sent by a man whose brother had been held for almost two years:

> 'Thank you for your e-mail and your concern about my brother. There is no change and no development in the case. And it is very difficult to visit him because he is now in Basra. And there are a lot of problems facing Sunnis who go to Basra in order to visit their relatives. Besides it is very difficult to get permission from American soldiers to visit him. And there isn't any charge. Now we lost the hope to get him again.'

The number of long-term detainees has reportedly increased since September 2005. According to the Iraqi Human Rights Ministry, on 28 September 2005 there were 1,443 detainees held by the Multinational Force for more than one year. However, according to figures provided by US officials, in early November 2005, among the nearly 13,900 detainees held by the Multinational Force there were some 3,800 who had by then been held for more than one year and more than 200 who had been held for more than two years.

Amnesty International knows of internees who at the beginning of 2006 had been held for more than two years without having been charged or tried. For example, **Kamal Muhammad 'Abdullah al-Jibouri**, a 43-year-old former soldier married with 11 children, continued to be held in early February 2006, after some two years in detention without charge or trial. He was detained on 5 February 2004 by US troops in the al-Khusum village of the Salaheddin governorate. He was held at Abu Ghraib prison initially, but transferred to Camp Bucca, near Basra, in May 2005. Since his transfer, it has become particularly difficult for his relatives to visit him. Two relatives of Kamal Muhammad 'Abdullah al-Jibouri, both aged about 40, were also detained by US troops on 5 February 2004 in al-Khusum village. At least one of the two was reportedly transferred at the end of 2005 to Fort Suse, near Suleimaniya in northern Iraq. As of February 2006, both men, like Kamal Muhammad 'Abdullah al-Jibouri, continued to be held without charge or trial.

Treatment of internees

Although the US authorities introduced various measures to safeguard prisoners after the Abu Ghraib prison scandal, there continue to be reports of torture or ill-treatment of detainees by US troops. In September 2005, several members of the US National Guard's 184th Infantry Regiment were sentenced to prison terms in connection with torture or ill-treatment of Iraqis who had reportedly been detained in March 2005 following an attack on a power plant near Baghdad. According to media reports, the abuse involved the use of an electro-shock gun on handcuffed and blindfolded detainees. The *Los Angeles Times* referred to a member of the battalion having reported that 'the stun gun was used on at least one man's testicles'.

The abuse was investigated after a soldier who was not involved in the mistreatment discovered film footage showing parts of the abuse on a laptop computer. At least twelve soldiers from the National Guard's 184th Infantry Regiment were charged with misconduct 'relating to abuse and maltreatment of detainees'. Three sergeants were sentenced to between five and twelve months of imprisonment and four other soldiers were sentenced to hard labour.

In another incident, five soldiers from the 75th Ranger Regiment were charged before a court martial in connection with allegations of detainee abuse. The case arose from an incident on 7 September 2005 when three detainees were allegedly punched and kicked by the five US soldiers as they were awaiting movement to a detention facility. On 21 December 2005, it was announced that the five soldiers had been sentenced to be confined for periods ranging from 30 days to six months and reductions in rank.

Amnesty International has noted that in the above cases, US officials have apparently taken swift action to investigate the allegations of abuse and to prosecute the perpetrators. However, given that torture or ill-treatment have continued, the organization is concerned that insufficient safeguards have been put in place in order to protect detainees from the recurrence of abuse.

Amnesty International has interviewed former detainees and relatives of detainees held by the Multinational Force about treatment of detainees after the handover of power in June 2004. In one reported incident an electro-shock gun (taser) was used against detainees in circumstances which violate international human rights law prohibiting torture or ill-treatment. According to an eye-witness, in November 2005 a US guard at Camp Bucca used a taser against two detainees while they were being transferred in a vehicle to a medical appointment within the detention facility, shocking one on the arm and the other on his abdomen.

Electro-shock weapons have been developed as a non-lethal force option to be used to control dangerous or combative individuals. Amnesty International considers that electro-shock weapons are inherently open to abuse as they can inflict severe pain without leaving substantial marks, and can further be used to inflict repeated shocks.

Under Coalition Provisional Authority Memorandum No. 3, the Multinational Force was required to ensure that conditions and standards in all of its internment facilities satisfy Section IV of the Fourth Geneva Convention, which sets out standards for the treatment of detainees, including in relation to food, hygiene and the provision of medical attention, as well as contact with the outside world and penal and disciplinary sanctions.

Article 119 of the Fourth Geneva Convention provides that internees may not be punished other than by fines, discontinuance of privileges, fatigue duties – which may only be 'in connection with the maintenance of the place of internment' and not exceed two hours daily – and confinement. Article 119 further provides: 'In no case shall disciplinary penalties be inhuman, brutal or dangerous for the health of internees. Account shall be taken of the internee's age, sex and state of health.'

Despite this, former internees have alleged that disciplinary or penal sanctions have been used which breach the above provisions of the Fourth Geneva Convention and appear also to constitute a violation of international human rights treaties prohibiting torture or ill-treatment. In particular, internees at Camp Bucca are alleged to have been exposed deliberately to extremes of both heat and cold, by being made to wait for hours in the heat of the sun while their accommodation was searched and forcibly showered with cold water and exposed to cold air conditioners.

Amnesty International has previously expressed concern to the US authorities regarding their use of a restraint chair for detainees in Iraq. On 28 October 2005,

John Moore of Getty Images photographed an individual – reportedly a juvenile detained in the maximum security section of Abu Ghraib prison – strapped into a four-point restraint chair. US Army military police reportedly said that he was being 'punished for disrespecting them' and would remain for two hours in the chair 'as punishment'.

The photograph showed the detainee tightly immobilized. He had straps across his chest and his wrists and ankles were bound, with his legs bent at the knee, and his head was thrown back. Such a position would appear to carry a significant health risk as well as cause discomfort and pain. Prolonged immobilization in restraints is known to carry a risk of blood clots or asphyxia. On 15 December 2005, Amnesty International wrote to the Multinational Force Task Force 134, which is responsible for Detainee Operations in Iraq, stating that the organization would 'consider the manner of restraint shown to amount to cruel, inhuman or degrading treatment and in violation of the US's obligations under international human rights treaties'.

In a letter of 17 January 2006, Major General John D. Gardner, commander of Multinational Force Task Force 134, responded to Amnesty International stating that 'in accordance with US Army policy, restraint cannot be used as a form of punishment'. He continued that a restraint chair may be used in order to gain control of a violent detainee. However, Amnesty International was informed that the incident was being investigated and that policies concerning the use of the restraint chair were under review. The use of the restraint chair has been suspended until the conclusions of this review.

Access to the outside world

Coalition Provisional Authority Memorandum No. 3 is deficient in several respects insofar as the question of access to detainees is concerned. In particular, while it provides for the International Committee of the Red Cross to have access to detainees, it qualifies this, stating that access by the International Committee of the Red Cross can be denied 'for reasons of imperative necessity as an exceptional and temporary measure'.

There are no regulations spelled out in the Memorandum regarding internees' right of access to relatives or legal counsel. It states that the provisions of section 4 of the Fourth Geneva Convention apply, which include some reference to contact with relatives and legal counsel, but it makes no reference to other international standards relating to the rights of detainees, such as The Body of Principles for the Protection of All Persons under Any Form of Detention or Imprisonment, and the Declaration on the Protection of All Persons From Enforced Disappearance.

Amnesty International is concerned that the Multinational Force's failure to guarantee detainees' access to the outside world, including to their families and to legal counsel, has been a contributory factor facilitating torture and ill-treatment and other human rights abuses of detainees. Such denial of access poses a continuing risk of further such abuses.

Visits by relatives

During the first weeks after arrest detainees held by US forces of the Multinational Force have no access to their families or legal counsel. According to the *Detainee visitation rules and guidelines* issued by the US military in July 2005, security internees are not entitled to receive visits during the first 60 days of internment.

US forces have imposed these restrictions also in high profile cases. For example, **Ali Omar Ibrahim Al-Mashhadani**, a 36-year-old cameraman for *Reuters* news agency, was arrested on 8 August 2005 in Ramadi by US forces after a search of his house. Reuters Global Managing Editor Director, David Schlesinger, protested the decision to detain the cameraman without any charges and the restrictions on his access to the outside world: 'I am shocked and appalled that such decision could be taken without his having access to legal counsel of his choosing, his family or his employers.' Despite this protest, Ali Omar Ibrahim Al-Mashhadani could not be visited before the expiry of the 60 days limit. His family visited him for the first time on 7 October 2005 at Abu Ghraib prison. He was transferred to Camp Bucca, near Basra, the same day. He was released in mid-January 2006 without having been charged or tried.

Internees held by the United Kingdom forces have also complained about delayed access to the outside world. **Hillal 'Abdul Razzaq 'Ali al-Jedda**, a 48-year-old dual national with UK and Iraqi citizenship, was arrested at his sister's house in Baghdad on 10 October 2004 by US troops who were accompanied by Iraqi security forces. He reported that during his arrest he was beaten, forced to the floor, hooded and tightly handcuffed, causing pain. At Baghdad Airport he was handed over to the United Kingdom forces and transferred to the UK-controlled Shu'aiba Divisional Temporary Detention Facility, near Basra. For the first 28 days of his detention he was reportedly held in solitary confinement in a small and badly ventilated cell. He claims that his family was only informed about his whereabouts 33 days after his detention. According to the United Kingdom authorities '[s]tandard operating practices require the Multinational Force to inform relatives of the detention of internees within 24 hours of their internment'.

Some relatives of detainees have told human rights organizations, including Amnesty International, that for weeks or months they were not able to establish the whereabouts of a detainee. The Christian Peacemaker Teams reported the case of **'Adnan Talib Hassan Al-'Unaibi**, an imam in the town of Hilla, who was detained by US forces on 1 May 2004 while attending a public meeting at the premises of a local human rights organization. During the raid US forces reportedly killed two people. After the detention a brother of the imam went to the Iraqi Assistance Centre in Baghdad to find out his whereabouts. However, the detention was only confirmed at the end of May 2004 after the brother had obtained more information from released detainees – including the prisoner's sequence number. Despite numerous inquiries, relatives were not able to establish 'Adnan Talib Hassan Al-'Unaibi's whereabouts for several months. They were only allowed to visit him after he had been in detention for five months. He was eventually released uncharged in September 2005.

In principle, internees are entitled to four visits per month or one visit per week after they have passed the first 60 days of detention. However, relatives have frequently reported that they were not able to conduct visits, because the detention facility was located far away and travelling long distances in Iraq is unsafe.

Visits by legal counsel

After the first 60 days of internment, internees are entitled to receive visits by legal counsel. Amnesty International has asked numerous relatives of internees, former internees, lawyers and human rights activists about the possibilities of security internees seeking the support of legal counsel. It appears that visits to security detainees by legal counsel are extremely rare. The main reason for this seems to be the belief that it is futile to seek legal counsel when the detainee will not be brought before a court of law. Former internees and lawyers alike have told Amnesty International they did not believe that a lawyer could have significantly furthered the case of a security internee.

Visits by monitoring bodies

As indicated earlier, Coalition Provisional Authority Memorandum No 3 in principle grants the International Committee for the Red Cross access to Multinational Force-held detainees at locations throughout the country. In practice, however, the International Committee for the Red Cross has been able to visit only a limited number of larger detention facilities, mostly due to security considerations. According to the International Committee of the Red Cross, in the period from May to September 2005 'the main detention/internment facilities covered during that period were Camp Cropper (Baghdad Airport); Camp Bucca near the southern town of Basra; and several detention places in Kurdistan'. According to the Multinational Force, the International Committee for the Red Cross has 'access to all Theater Internment Facilities in the theatre'. Amnesty International understands from this that the International Committee for the Red Cross does not have access to brigade and division internment facilities of the Multinational Force – that is, military bases where detainees are mainly held during the first days or weeks of their detention.

Therefore, in many locations of detention under Multinational Force control, no independent body is currently able to monitor the treatment of detainees held by the Multinational Force. Yet, visits to places of detention by independent monitoring bodies are an important safeguard for persons deprived of their liberty. Visits enable experts to examine at first hand the conditions of detention and treatment of detainees and to make recommendations for improvements. Visits can have a deterrent effect against abuse and provide a necessary link for detainees with the outside world.

According to the United Kingdom authorities, the International Committee for the Red Cross has 'full and unrestricted access' to its detention facilities in Iraq and the International Committee for the Red Cross has described conditions of internment as 'generally good'.

The Iraqi Human Rights Ministry is conducting periodic visits to detention facilities under the control of the Multinational Force. The ministry has opened an office at Abu Ghraib prison which is also monitoring the situation of internees held by the Multinational Force. The ministry is circulating regular reports on its monitoring activities concerning the situation of detainees in Iraq. An official of the ministry told Amnesty International that its monitoring includes occasional visits to brigade and division internment facilities of the Multinational Force.

Several UN human rights experts have faced obstacles in their attempts to visit detainees held by the US forces – including those held in Iraq. In a statement issued on 18 November 2005, five independent experts of the UN Commission on Human Rights – including the Chairperson-Rapporteur of the Working Group on Arbitrary Detention and the Special Rapporteur on Torture and other Cruel, Inhuman or Degrading Treatment or Punishment – expressed their regret about the US refusal of terms for a fact finding mission to the US detention facility at Guantánamo Bay, Cuba. This statement followed a letter of 25 June 2004 and several follow-up letters sent by UN human rights experts to the US authorities requesting to visit 'those persons arrested, detained or tried on grounds of alleged terrorism or other violations, in Iraq, Afghanistan, the Guantánamo Bay military base and elsewhere'. At the time of writing, none of the five UN human rights experts had been able to visit US detention facilities in Iraq.

Secret and unacknowledged detention

The US has held an unknown number of persons detained in Iraq without any contact with the outside world in violation of international standards. These so called 'ghost detainees' were largely hidden to prevent the International Committee of the Red Cross from visiting them.

On 17 June 2004, US Defense Secretary Donald H. Rumsfeld admitted that in November 2003 he ordered military officials to detain a senior member of Ansar al-Islam without listing him in the prison's register. This prisoner was reportedly arrested in late June or early July 2003 and was transferred to an undisclosed location outside Iraq. He was returned to Iraq where he was detained in secret until May 2004 without being registered or assigned a prison register number.

There are indications that persons detained in Iraq have secretly been transferred outside Iraq for interrogation by the CIA. For example, **Hassan Ghul**, a Pakistani national reportedly detained in January 2004 in northern Iraq, is according to Human Rights Watch possibly held in CIA custody. According to a report in the Swiss newspaper, *Der Sonntagsblick*, a confidential communication of the Egyptian Foreign Ministry to its embassy in London intercepted by the Swiss secret service, stated that Egyptian intelligence could confirm that 23 Iraqi and Afghan citizens have been interrogated by US intelligence agents at the military air base Mihael Kogalniceanu in Romania. The communication further stated that similar interrogation centres existed in the Ukraine, Kosovo, Macedonia and Bulgaria.

In at least one incident US officials have tried to cover up the death of an unacknowledged detainee in Iraq. **Mandel al-Jamadi** was detained by US troops and placed in Abu Ghraib prison where he died on 4 November 2003 as an unregistered detainee. Documents obtained by the American Civil Liberties Union under the US Freedom of Information Act, suggest that Mandel al-Jamadi died due to 'blunt force injuries complicated by compromised respiration'.

US officials have defended the practice of denying detainees access to the International Committee of the Red Cross for purposes of 'imperative military necessity'. Under Article 143 of the Fourth Geneva Convention, the International Committee of the Red Cross visits to civilian internees may be denied 'for reasons of imperative military necessity', but 'only as an exceptional and temporary measure'. In Iraq in January 2004, the US authorities invoked 'military necessity' when they refused to grant the International Committee of the Red Cross access to eight detainees held in Abu Ghraib. According to the Fay report, one of the eight detainees, a Syrian national, was at that time held in a tiny dark cell without windows, toilet or bedding. The inhumane treatment of this Syrian detainee, facilitated by the invocation of 'military necessity', was not limited to solitary confinement in harsh conditions. Around 18 December 2003, he was abused and threatened with dogs. According to the US military, there is a photograph of him kneeling on the floor with his hands tied behind his back, while an unmuzzled dog is snarling a few feet from his face. During an International Committee of the Red Cross visit in mid-March 2004, the organization's delegates were again denied access to him, and other detainees, on the grounds of 'military necessity'. In January and March 2004, the International Committee of the Red Cross questioned the 'exceptional and temporary' nature of the denial of access. By the time of its March visit, the Syrian detainee had been held incommunicado and under interrogation for four months.

US military investigations have suggested that up to 100 so-called ghost detainees may have been held in US detention facilities in Iraq. However, the Church report summary of March 2005 stated that 'the practice of Department of Defense holding "ghost detainees" has now ceased'.

The practice of holding detainees in secret, with no contact with the outside world, places the person outside the protection of the law, denying them important safeguards and leaving them vulnerable to torture and ill-treatment. They have no access to lawyers, families or doctors. They are often kept in prolonged arbitrary detention without charge or trial. They are unable to challenge their arrest or detention, whose lawfulness is not assessed by any judge or similar authority. Their treatment and conditions are not monitored by any independent body, national or international. The secrecy of their detention allows the concealment of any further human rights violations they suffer, including torture or ill-treatment, and allows governments to evade accountability.

In certain circumstances, when people are held in secret detention and the authorities refuse to disclose their fate or whereabouts, they have 'disappeared'. This practice, known as enforced disappearance, is expressly prohibited under international law. International law requires that any person deprived of their liberty must be held in an officially recognized place of detention.

Enforced disappearance violates the rules of international law which provide for, among others, the right to recognition as a person before the law, the right to liberty and security of the person, and the right not to be subjected to torture or other ill-treatment. It also violates – or constitutes a grave threat to – the right to life. In certain circumstances, enforced disappearance can also be a crime against humanity.

International human rights bodies have held that secret detention and enforced disappearances themselves constitute ill-treatment or torture, in view of the considerable suffering of persons detained without contact with their families or anyone else from the outside world, and without knowing when or even if they will ever be freed or allowed to see their families again.

The same is true for the suffering caused to family members of 'disappeared' persons. In a number of cases, international human rights bodies have held that the authorities' denial of their right to know what has happened to their relatives has violated the prohibition of torture and ill-treatment.

Internment of women and children

Coalition Provisional Authority Memorandum No.3 includes provisions for the internment of children: 'Any person under the age of 18 interned at any time shall in all cases be released not later than 12 months after the initial date of internment'.

According to the United Kingdom authorities, there are no UK or US detention facilities allocated for women or children in Iraq. They further stated that at US detention facilities women and juveniles are segregated from adult males unless they are members of the same family. As of October 2005, United Kingdom authorities were not holding any women or children in detention.

At the end of September 2005 there were about 200 juveniles held by the Multinational Force who were scheduled to be transferred shortly to the jurisdiction of the Iraqi Ministry of Labour and Social Affairs. The newspaper *al-Sharq al-Awsat* reported in December 2005 that the Iraqi Judicial Council had appointed a judge to deal specifically with cases of detained juveniles held by the Multinational Force.

At the end of January 2006, a US military spokesman announced the release of five woman detainees, while four others remained held by the US forces.

'High Value' Detainees

The vast majority of detainees who were held or continue to be held by the Multinational Force without charge or trial are so called 'security internees'– that is, persons detained in the context of the ongoing armed conflict. In addition, US forces continue to hold so-called high value detainees – a category which has mainly been used for persons with senior positions under Saddam Hussain's government. Coalition Provisional Authority Order No. 99 refers to a Memorandum of Understanding between the Multinational Force and Iraqi authorities regarding "the handling of High Value Detainees." Amnesty

International requested a copy of that document from the US government, but to date has not received this.

At least two 'high value' detainees have died in custody under circumstances suggesting that torture or ill-treatment caused or contributed to their deaths. **'Abd Hamad Mawoush**, a major general in the Iraqi army under Saddam Hussain, died in US detention on 26 November 2003 after having a sleeping bag forced over his head and body and one of his interrogators sat on his chest. On 23 January 2006, a US court martial convicted a US army interrogator of his killing and sentenced the soldier to forfeit $6,000 of his salary. **Muhammad Mun'im al-Izmerly**, a 65-year-old chemical scientist, was detained in April 2003 and taken to Camp Cropper where he died in January 2004. An autopsy report found that he 'died from a sudden hit to his head'.

The group of 'high value' detainees included former prisoners of war who are now standing trial. Some former prisoners of war, including Saddam Hussain, have been referred to the Supreme Iraqi Criminal Tribunal (formerly known as Iraqi Special Tribunal). Although standing before an Iraqi court, Saddam Hussain and several others continue to be held in the custody of the Multinational Force at the request of the Iraqi authorities.

According to Multinational Force Task Force 134, in mid-February 2006 thirteen "high value" detainees continue to be held without charge or trial. Their cases were said to be subject to review by the High Value Detainee Special Review Committee, described as a 'U.S. Government panel staffed by military and civilian security and intelligence specialists qualified to assess security threat, as well as by representatives of the Regime Crimes Liaison office, which acts in support of the Iraqi Higher Tribunal'.

Earlier, the US government stated in its report to the UN Committee Against Torture, that US forces in Iraq were holding a 'small number of enemy prisoners of war'. These apparently included persons who had been detained as prisoners of war between March 2003 and June 2004, and therefore should have been released or charged at the end of the occupation on 28 June 2004.

Amnesty International calls on the Iraqi Authorities and the international community to ensure that all persons who have been responsible for human rights violations under the government of Saddam Hussain are brought to justice in trials conforming to international standards. However, according to Amnesty International's information – nearly three years after the demise of Saddam Hussain's government – some former officials of that government continue to be held without charge or trial.

Most of the 'high value' detainees – if not all of them – are currently being held at Camp Cropper, a detention facility of the US forces near Baghdad Airport. Relatives of 'high value' detainees have reported restrictions on visits. According to a former detainee at Camp Cropper, visits by relatives are generally only allowed once every three months. For example, **Huda Salih Mehdi 'Ammash**, the only female member of the Revolutionary Command Council under Saddam Hussain's government, was reportedly permitted family visits on only four occasions during her detention from May 2003 until November 2005.

In December 2005, several 'high value' detainees were released without having been charged or tried. They included two women scientists, namely (the above mentioned) Huda Salih Mehdi 'Ammash and **Rihab Rashid Taha**. Both had been held in US detention for about 30 months.

Amnesty's recommendations arising from this report, together with the references to it, are available online (www.amnesty.org).

SEEKING MISSING PERSONS IN IRAQ

Eman Ahmad Khamas, an Iraqi journalist who lives in Baghdad, was interviewed by Amy Goodman on 6 March on the Democracy Now! radio programme in the United States.

EMAN AHMAD KHAMAS: ... I work on the missing, a very big issue in Iraq, I work on the detainees. People disappear in Iraq. People – especially men – are arrested, and you don't hear anything about them. For example, during the first days of the war, between 20 March and 9 April [2003], when the Iraqi state collapsed, people disappeared. There are eyewitnesses that these people were taken by the American troops. Some of them may be killed. Some of them may be in jail. But now, they don't exist.

AMY GOODMAN: Well, how do you find out? I mean, if you want to find out if someone has been jailed, what do you do?

EMAN AHMAD KHAMAS: There are eyewitnesses in the place that he disappeared, and they say that 'We saw him, he was injured and was taken in an American tank or vehicle,' or 'He was taken,' ... There are injured prisoners who are released and they say that in our room and the place, we had this man, and they give his description – many things that no one else would know, only the person who was with him.

AMY GOODMAN: The American authorities in the US-run prisons will not tell you?

EMAN AHMAD KHAMAS: We go to the American military bases, to the prisons, and we ask about these people. They deny them.

AMY GOODMAN: They deny that they are there?

EMAN AHMAD KHAMAS: They deny they exist in that prison. For example, we have a story of a man. He was supposed to be in prison in Umm Qasr, you know, Camp Bucca in the south, deep in the south.

AMY GOODMAN: Camp Bucca is named for a fireman who was killed 9/11 in New York.

EMAN AHMAD KHAMAS: Yes, but for Iraqis it is a very big prison. It is a camp where tens of thousands of Iraqis are arrested for three years now. So people come from there, and they say, 'We know this man, we know this man,' etc. And we go there. Sometimes even the American themselves, they say – the American authorities, the American officials, they say, yes, they put list of names. And when we go back, we ask about them, they say, 'No, we didn't do that.' And we show them, I have a paper, I have a document, of one of these men. And now he's denied.

I don't know the number of these people. The number is between 5,000 and 15,000. But I had a meeting with a general called General Brandenburg in the Ministry of Justice. And he said that he has records of that period. And he asked me to give him the names that I'm looking for. And I did. But when we had the meeting, and we had a date to go and to talk about these people, to give him the names, he did not show up, unfortunately. I'm still waiting for an answer. They said, in the Ministry of Justice, they said that he's changed. Now, there is another one, called Garner. But I didn't meet him yet. And I'm looking forward to meeting him and giving him the list of names and the stories of these people who disappeared.

This is a very big tragedy in Iraq, because there are families, mothers, wives, children, who are waiting to hear about their loved ones, if they exist, if they are dead, if they are alive. They simply won't answer. That's all ...

'STRIVE FOR CONCERTED NUCLEAR DISARMAMENT'

Pope Benedict XVI exposed the fallacy of seeking security through nuclear weapons in his New Year Message, from which these excerpts are taken.

'... It must not be forgotten that, tragically, violent fratricidal conflicts and devastating wars still continue to sow tears and death in vast parts of the world. Situations exist where conflict, hidden like flame beneath ashes, can flare up anew and cause immense destruction. Those authorities who, rather than making every effort to promote peace, incite their citizens to hostility towards other nations, bear a heavy burden of responsibility: in regions particularly at risk, they jeopardize the delicate balance achieved at the cost of patient negotiations and thus help make the future of humanity more uncertain and ominous. What can be said, too, about those governments which count on nuclear arms as a means of ensuring the security of their countries? Along with countless persons of good will, one can state that this point of view is not only baneful but also completely fallacious. In a nuclear war there would be no victors, only victims. The truth of peace requires that all – whether those governments which openly or secretly possess nuclear arms, or those planning to acquire them – agree to change their course by clear and firm decisions, and strive for a progressive and concerted nuclear disarmament. The resources which would be saved could then be employed in projects of development capable of benefiting all their people, especially the poor.

In this regard, one can only note with dismay the evidence of a continuing growth in military expenditure and the flourishing arms trade, while the political and juridical process established by the international community for promoting disarmament is bogged down in general indifference. How can there ever be a future of peace when investments are still made in the production of arms and in research aimed at developing new ones? It can only be hoped that the international community will find the wisdom and courage to take up once more, jointly and with renewed conviction, the process of disarmament, and thus concretely ensure the right to peace enjoyed by every individual and every people. By their commitment to safeguarding the good of peace, the various agencies of the international community will regain the authority needed to make their initiatives credible and effective.

The first to benefit from a decisive choice for disarmament will be the poor countries, which rightly demand, after having heard so many promises, the concrete implementation of their right to development ...'

VANUNU REPORTS

Mordechai Vanunu, who blew the whistle on the Israeli nuclear weapons programme, has been harassed by the Israeli authorities ever since his release from prison in 2004. He sent this account of a day in court in March 2006.

'Today, the trial continued at 13:00, in the same court in Jerusalem. Mr Feldman could not come to the hearing so Michael Sfard was my lawyer. Few supporters were with me in the court. Jerry Levin was there plus three people from Norway and one from Belgium. No press or any media people. The judge was Mr Yoel Zur, who already this week gave a decision that the court will not accept all the evidence from the Internet and from 'Internet Chats' taken without any authority from my computer by the police.

Sfard cross-examined the policeman Peterburg, who interrogated me months ago in the police station. He especially asked about his methods of going through my computers to see my e-mails and chats, and going to court to ask for my arrest, and permission to search my room. Sfard proved to the court, according to the police documents, that they asked Microsoft to give them details of my Hotmail account, my passwords, and the internet protocol address. All this was after the police went to the court, asking the judge for the right to go to my e-mails.

Microsoft obeyed these orders and gave them all the details, but not the passwords. This took place on 12 August 2004, three months before arresting me and taking my computers. Sfard pointed out that it is strange to ask Microsoft to give this information before they have the court's order to listen to my private conversations. It means they wanted to go to my e-mails in secret or maybe even help the secret services, Shaback and Mossad, but not as the police stated, by Peterburg, that he went to my e-mail account and all his material came only from my computer.

The most important revelation was that the police each time went to the court claiming that I was suspected of spying activity, not with just breaking my restrictions. So Mr Sfard asked the police to tell the court what kind of espionage I was involved in. The policeman did not have any answers and said that he brought all the evidence to the court. When Sfard asked again about any material related to the 'espionage' accusation, Peterburg had no answers.

It was also revealed that the state came to the court with two special secret Government orders, which allowed the prosecution to keep documents related to the court hearing secret. One was from the Minister of Internal Security and one from the Minister of Defence. What is this about? We don't know. One thing is clear – the secret cooperation between the police and Shaback/Mossad.

So Sfard proved that the police had misled the judges with false accusations; who then gave orders to arrest me, to search my room, to go to my e-mail, confiscate my computers (for almost a year), and also mislead Microsoft to believe they are helping in a case of espionage, otherwise Microsoft would not have cooperated with such orders? All this case, interrogations, arrests, confiscations of private properties and more, all done from the start under the false and misleading statements to the courts of "suspicion of espionage", and yet they are not charging me with spy crimes.

The judge also asked questions. He wanted to know what the police said to the judges when they asked for all these orders, and how the proceedings had been conducted. Peterburg, most of the time, said he did not remember. It looked like he did not want to answer a lot of questions. The prosecutor wants the court to have the tapes, where they video me in secret when I was interrogated by the police in their offices. The court decided to give time until May 1st, for each side to write their arguments for and against "No case to answer". Meanwhile, there will be other hearings between now and then.

That was it for today. Please, anyone who could suggest prominent names who could testify on the subject of freedom of expression and hopefully could come to testify or write on the matter etc? Any ideas or help in this matter, my right to freedom of speech, and that I have not committed any crimes, including donations for legal expenses, would be very welcome. Thank You.'

The fighting back union

Transport and General Workers' Union

TONY WOODLEY
General Secretary

JACK DROMEY
Deputy General Secretary

JIMMY KELLY
Chair – GEC

BRENDA SANDERS
Vice Chair – GEC

Bring the troops home from Iraq

tel: 020 7611 2500   www.tgwu.org.uk   fax: 020 7611 2555

Red Pepper Magazine For resources to help change the world

www.redpepper.org.uk

red pepper — raising the political temperature

12 month subscription for just £20 PLUS our three most recent special issues AND a copy of Tariq Ali's 'Rough Music: Blair, Bombs, Baghdad, London, Terror' FREE

Don't miss out on our forthcoming issues, including

- On the road with the Zapatistas
- Religion and the Left
- Hail to the Chief: exclusive interview with the Venezuelan army commander
- Selling sickness: examination of Big Pharma

Offer includes three special issues (worth £7.50)

 Special issue on Palestine

 Rotten to the Core: Education special

 Health special: Why market reform is bad for your health

Save £9 off our standard subscription rate at www.redpepper.org.uk/spokesman or call our Subscriber Hotline on 01296 487493 and quote reference SP/1

Offer ends 30 April 06

Design for a New Europe

John Gillingham
University of Missouri, St. Louis

'...a remarkable account of the most recent developments in the European Union...rethinks the process of European integration and offers an original prescription on how to reconfigure it...should be considered in any serious debate about the further course of European integration.'
Václav Klaus, President of the Czech Republic

Publication April 2006
£35.00 | HB   £12.99 | PB

'...a convincing diagnosis of the EU's present malaise and a challenging set of prescriptions...'
Sir Geoffrey Owen, Senior Fellow, Institute of Management, London School of Economics

'...a lucid, well-written account of what is wrong with the EU and how it can be fixed. It is a must-read for Europhiles and Eurosceptics alike.'
Tom Zwart, University of Utrecht School of Law

www.cambridge.org/currentaffairs

CAMBRIDGE UNIVERSITY PRESS

Reviews

Media Myth

David Edwards & David Cromwell, *The Guardians of Power: The Myth of the Liberal Media*, Pluto Press, 256 pages, hardback ISBN 0745324835 £45, paperback ISBN 0745324827 £14.99

Was that really 30 years ago? Reading the first chapter of *Guardians of Power* by David Edwards and David Cromwell of the monitoring group Media Lens (www.medialens.org), I recalled a similar exercise in media analysis by the Glasgow University Media Group. It was an attempt to measure and explain the manufacture of news by television companies and had the title *Bad News* – they also conducted the follow-up called *Really Bad News,* published six years later, which depressingly showed that little had changed.

At the time of the publication of *Bad News* I worked as a film and video cameraman, and I can reveal that its appearance caused no small anguish amongst the editorial staff of the day. Personally I had been aware that the pictures I recorded did not necessarily relate to the commentary or context in which they were transmitted. By this time I had already read James Halloran's case study on *Demonstrations and Communication,* which had alerted me to cultural and other powers that affected the selection of topics and the news angle taken for these topics, as well as the need for a differentiated audience to decode the mixture of pictures, sounds, language, and authoritative sources dependent on their level of empathy with the actors. When *Bad News* was published it gave me the momentum to study the topic more because I was part of the events that were being studied – in particular, the dustcart drivers' strike in Glasgow, where the Labour Council, supported by a Labour Government, used troops to break the strike.

The authors of *Bad News* had great difficulties to overcome. Quantifying news coverage is an extraordinarily difficult task. You can be accused of a simplistic approach if you quantify television output by aggregating the transmission times of individual items under specific headings, or you can expend a great deal of effort in a more contextual and qualitative analysis. A further difficulty for the team was that they would have to wait for a year before their work was published in book form, so that it had no direct effect on the subject under examination. I mention this because in *Guardians of Power* similar tasks have been undertaken with respect to the written word. But, spooling forward 30 years, personal computers, search engines and the internet have provided its authors with a tool of immense power for such a task.

Media Lens' great strength is the way in which it pools the breadth of its subscribers to scan the news in print and on the web so that when someone notices a significant piece of news, or a blatant distortion in a report, they can raise the alert which draws the attention of everyone accessing the service. The brainpower, computing power and sheer weight of activists such a system can call upon is huge. Instead of analysis being passed serial fashion along the line, it proceeds in a cascade, multiplying contacts in seconds. Importantly this system requires the active engagement of some, but not necessarily all, of those who read the alert.

One pertinent example from *Guardians of Power* is the alert that Blair and Straw were lying about the withdrawal of the UN arms inspectors from Iraq. Both said that Saddam Hussein had thrown them out, yet there are many official sources that flatly contradict this. Further, when war was about to start, several newspapers carried the same disinformation in a compilation of justifications for war. Within minutes, earlier reports, filed by the same correspondents, that withdrawal of the arms inspectors came after a warning from the United States that its bombing operation, Desert Fox, was about to start and that the inspectors' safety could not be guaranteed, had been retrieved from various archives, and brought to the attention of these forgetful journalists in particular, and the media in general.

The power of this informal network is the message from this little book. Each alert that goes out informs but also, as a subtext, it asks is this true, can this be contradicted, and better still, can it be contradicted by its own author? Within its network Media Lens has a broad range of active visitors who all bring something to the party. Thus an article on Kosovo may be read by only a handful of visitors to the site, but it will more than likely be read by those with an interest in the topic, thus providing a bank of knowledge of its history and the history of reports on Kosovo as a news topic. This could mean that waiting in the inbox for the journalist before he or she arrives at the desk on the day following publication of the erroneous article, they will find polite e-mails asking if they remember that article which they filed three years ago in which the migration of refugees from Kosovo happened after NATO started bombing and not prior, as is now reported.

A lesson that can be drawn from this is that news organisations do allow breaking news to be reported as it happens. It is when the significance of this news becomes apparent, and questions arise as to how it fits in to the corporate editorial line of an organisation, that bias is mobilized and the gatekeepers on the flow of information swing into operation. It is at this time that the gate guarding the original source is closed, and that from official and approved sources is held wide-open. When challenged on omissions in their coverage, news organizations can invariably draw attention to the fact that their previous reports did carry the alleged omission and therefore they have covered it. This neatly sidesteps the fact that, without the original information as a prefix, the story is now set in a different context. What is invidious about this process is that from now on the story is invariably set in its new and distorted context, thus masking the history of the events in question.

Bias can enter the news gathering system at many junctions. Edwards and Cromwell rightly point to the capitalist structures of the corporations that now own the satellites and instruct and direct the crews to various locations which interest them as corporations, and also as competitors, where being first to break the news or, say, report an exclusive story, really matters to them. The development of Media Lens may permit it soon to have the power to act as an alternative source and a correcting influence on the gross distortions in the news we receive at present. The authors do give a lead in their references to 'The Corporation' because, through Media Lens, they have hit upon a weapon to use against those who wish to distort and control the flow of information and knowledge. Some time spent on their thoughts on the development of this tool would have given extra bite to their text. It is this that I believe is the best contribution they can make to the debate. Their call at the end of the book for 'full human dissent' is welcome, but I feel somewhat blunted by their fascination for Erich Fromm, who takes a far less conflictual view of the world than many others who have provided a critique of the 'Myth of the Liberal Media', which was well dissected up to the 1980s when the Left lost its way.

Perhaps it is time to dust down Wright Mills' and Dahl's analyses of power with élites versus pluralism, which lead to the more interesting work of Bachrach and Baratz in the United States and Steven Lukes in the United Kingdom. The latter's radical view explains the phenomena so well exposed in *Guardians of Power*. He did receive criticism at the time for his concept of 'latent conflict', which some equated to the Marxist concept of 'false consciousness'. But that was where I came into this debate. How could it be, I thought, that a family watching the news in a council estate I had been filming can accept as incontestable a report providing an ideologically loaded solution to social and economic problems which would not benefit them? It wasn't that 'there is no alternative'; it was that the solution on offer was the preferred solution of the owners of the technical and financial apparatus that controlled the media system. The financial threshold to enter this club and provide an alternative was set so high that the alternative can, to all intents and purposes, be excluded.

Could Media Lens have found the practical answer to the above dilemmas through the internet? I believe a solution is to be found in there somewhere.

Henry McCubbin is a founder member of scottishleftreview.org,
an internet journal of the Left in Scotland.

Sage with Clay Feet

Andrew Brown, *J. D. Bernal – The Sage of Science*, Oxford University Press, 576 pages, hardback ISBN 0198515448 £25.00

Desmond Bernal earned a reputation as a Titan among British scientists, and a distinguished boffin for the British armed forces in the Second World War. Together with Solly Zuckerman and others, he pioneered the study of the effects of bombing on cities.

His biographer tells us that Bernal's '*pièce de résistance* was the planning of D-Day: a contribution that has given rise to some controversy'. He earned the nickname 'Sage' because he was believed to know everything. But this belief was an exaggeration, even if he did know a great many things. Among Communist scientists, Joseph Needham knew a great deal more, and carried his knowledge with a great deal less dogmatic assurance.

This is a fine biography, and it is not averse to painting at least some of the warts as well as the achievements of its subject. Desmond Bernal was a pioneer of X-ray crystallography, and laid the foundation of molecular biology. He was a generalist, and wrote stimulating analyses of the social functions of science.

He was also an Irish rebel brought up under the shadow of the Easter Uprising, and became a committed Communist with a strong tendency to piety.

Bernal was one of the core group of British scientists who attended the Second International Congress of the History of Science and Technology in London. This was 'galvanised by the unexpected arrival of a delegation from the Soviet Union'. Eight contributors were led by Nikolai Bukharin, and his team included the distinguished geneticist, Vavilov. At the time the most powerful contribution of the group was esteemed to be a lecture by Boris Hessen, on the social and economic roots of Newton's *Principia*.

The unique flavour of the Russian contribution was described in *The Spectator* by Bernal, who had a female connection with the journal. (Bernal had several female connections, so much so that his archive of six boxes of his love letters is sealed, we are informed, until 2021, by which time, we may anticipate, at least some of the passion contained in them may be spent.)

We might wish that the archive could have included the Sage's thoughts about Bukharin and Vavilov, both of whom perished in Stalin's witch-hunts. In fact, Bernal gave his support to the charlatan academician Lysenko, who wrote perhaps the most dismal page in the history of Soviet Science.

Of course, by this time, Bernal was a luminary of the World Peace Committee, and one of the most distinguished sycophants of Stalin. There is a revealing description of a visit to China, which shows how the affection for Stalin carried over into support for Khrushchev. During a firework display at the Gate of Heavenly Peace, Bernal was approached by a tall Russian who said 'Nikita Sergeyevich wants to speak to you'. Bernal also met Zhou Enlai, who promised him an interview. But after the meeting with Khrushchev, Zhou sent 'an undiplomatic message … saying that he did not see any value in seeing him'.

Here was a man celebrated by Francis Crick as 'a genius' and by Linus Pauling as 'one of the greatest intellectuals of the twentieth century' and variously described as 'one of the best, if not the best, scientific minds in the world', and 'the pioneer who pushed the frontier forward', who could nonetheless embrace with all the fervour of a Moonie, a political creed of remarkable vacuity.

How could it all happen? Andrew Brown gives us an honest portrait, and shows us how very clever 'Sage' really was. But he does not hide the grosser lapses of the political man.

For this reason, although this is a very good book, it will not be the last. Quite aside from any indiscretions which may await us in the six sealed boxes of love letters, the circle of Sage's brilliance and incomprehension remains to be squared.

Ken Coates

Taking Mao Seriously

John Gittings, *The Changing Face of China: From Mao to Market*, **Oxford University Press, 372 pages, hardback ISBN 0192806122 £18.99**

In a footnote to the Introduction to this important new book on China, John Gittings, who was for many years *The Guardian* Asia correspondent and China staffer, writes *inter alia* as follows;

> 'In writing this general account of modern Chinese history since the Communist revolution, I have sought to give full value to the ideas and goals of the period when Mao was in power as well as charting the huge changes which have taken place since his death and particularly since the early 1990s ... There is no question that we know now much more about Mao's despotic behaviour and that it reflects very badly on him, even if there is room for argument over the reliability and veracity of some memoirs and recollections. However, I continue to believe that Mao was an original thinker whose arguments should be taken seriously and that the history of post-1949 China cannot be understood if he is regarded simply as a "monster" or as a despot only interested in the exercise of supreme power. Similarly I do not think that it is helpful to dismiss the "Cultural Revolution" simply as "ten years of chaos", attributable to power-hungry opportunists who exploited Mao's cult ... My own view remains that even in the area of ideology circumstances can alter cases – as indeed was shown by the speed with which Mao responded when the US eventually sought détente with China in the 1970s. Beijing's earlier efforts to open a diplomatic dialogue with the US in the mid-1950s also need to be accounted for. I remain convinced that "Western" (effectively American) hostility to a Communist-led China was an important contributory factor in the growth of Maoist extremism in the late 1950s and 1960s.'

How far then does the history, as Gitttings tells it, of this momentous half century in which China emerged from a semi-colonial state into a great industrial world power support his general conclusion? There can be no question that Mao sought unsuccessfully to win US neutrality in the civil war of 1946-9 and that Mao dismissed Beijing's anti-US propaganda in the early 1970s as 'firing off empty cannons' and immediately welcomed Nixon's offer of détente. The decision up till then of the United States not even to recognize the Government of mainland China, and to deal with the government of Taiwan as if it represented China, could not fail to generate extreme nationalism and a sense of isolation, in which the concept emerged of a 'gradual road' of development without outside help even, after the late 1960s, from the Soviet Union. Mao's thinking about the 'gradual road' did no more than reflect the actual facts of the world which China faced.

While the exaggerated expectations of the Great Leap Forward of the late 1950s undoubtedly led to near starvation and possibly millions of deaths, the twenty years of the People's Communes cannot be written off as a total disaster. Gittings supplies evidence to support the view that 'the specialised farming and rural industry of the 1980s derived some benefit from the earlier collective efforts of the rural work force when it was organized into communes, brigades and teams … that current achievements were based upon labour-intensive "capital construction" investment in land improvement of the 1960s and 1970s, but under the previous system could never have been realised.' William Hinton, author of *Fanshen*, the classic account of earlier land reform, is quoted by Gittings as arguing 'It is unlikely that if the collectives had been given the same autonomy in production and freedom to develop markets that private producers now enjoy, they would have lagged behind'. My own visit to China in 1978 with an invited medical mission left me impressed rather than otherwise with the several communes we visited, and I was not surprised to read that in a UNICEF publication of 2000 ' the Mother and Child Health network was greatly weakened after the Peoples Communes were abolished'.

Mao's promotion of the 'Cultural Revolution' raises more complex issues, in which Mao's age and health must be taken into account. A sense of frustration at slow progress and bureaucratic delays was widespread in the mid-1960s, especially among the increasingly large number of students. The 1981 Resolution on Mao's mistakes passed at the Eleventh Plenum of the Communist Party – five years after Mao's death – identified three causes behind the Cultural Revolution – first, Mao's failure to accept criticism and to realize what was being done behind his back by Lin Biao and the Gang of Four; second, the Chinese tradition of 'feudal autocracy' to which the Communist Party largely succumbed; third, the Party's birth and maturation during decades of war and 'fierce class struggle' had made it ill equipped to deal with the more subtle contradictions of a peaceful society, this weakness being exacerbated by the split with the Soviet Union.

This leaves untreated the crucial question of democracy in the Party and the ultimate division of the Party on this issue leading to the tragedy of Tiananmen Square in June of 1989 when, according to what Gittings calls the most reliable estimates, around a thousand protesters were killed and many more injured and brutally treated thereafter. Gittings makes it clear that the divisions in the Party were real and witnesses the presence of Zhao Ziyang among the students and workers in the Square and his replacement as Premier by Li Peng; the hesitancy, moreover, of the army at first to move, and the several days before the decision was reached to suppress the protests. The old guard of the Party saw a student victory as foreshadowing the end of the Party's rule, and was prepared to sacrifice many hundreds of lives to save their dominant position, but this was not the position of a possible majority of the Party members who supported Zhao Ziyang. Many references are made by Gittings to the strength of not only worker and student opposition but that of journalists and intellectuals, and particularly to the role of Professor Su Shaozhi, the path-breaking intellectual who had been head of the Institute of Marx, Lenin and Mao Tse Tung Thought in Beijing. Su Shaozhi spoke out at the time of the occupation of the Square against bureaucratisation and sectarianism. The Bertrand Russell Peace Foundation had made contact with him in the 1980s, and seen to it that his book on *Democratisation and Reform* was published by the Spokesman Press in 1988. Professor Su believed that democratisation was necessary and possible in China, and suffered exile for his beliefs.

Deng Xiaoping's subsequent return to power, in Gitttings' view, 'demonstrates yet again how the Chinese system still required a great leader to make it function'. The gap that had opened up between the people and the Party was closed by accelerated economic growth, which was providing employment for the millions who were pouring into the cities from the countryside. Deng could then argue that 'there was nothing inherently capitalistic about encouraging market forces, nothing wrong with allowing the rich to get richer, eventually (but not too soon) paying more taxes to help the poor'. 'The "non-public ownership sector" had become "an important component part" of China's socialist economy.'

The emergence of China as a major industrial power with massive international investment, and the domination of world markets for manufactures as a result of China's combination of advanced technology and cheap labour leaves, as Gittings clearly demonstrates, many problems unsolved apart from the lack of democracy. There is the widening gap between town and country and of living standards between rich and poor – millionaires at one extreme, slave labour at the other. There is a huge environmental problem of pollution, increasing dependence on imported oil, the threat of the Three Gorges dam to the surrounding countryside, and the rapid growth of the AIDS epidemic; and this is not to mention a possible collapse of the American market, to which so much of China's production is directed. Gittings starts his Introduction by looking forward to the 2008 Olympics which are to be held in China, and which some doomsters believe will be an environmental disaster. Gittings, as always throughout this book, takes a moderate view, not over-optimistic but not alarmist.

Michael Barratt Brown

Foot on Paine

Trevor Griffiths, *These Are The Times – A Life of Thomas Paine,* Spokesman Books, 208 pages, paperback ISBN 0851246958 £15.00
Bernard Vincent, *The Transatlantic Republican – Thomas Paine and the Age of Revolutions*, Amsterdam Monographs in American Studies, Editions Rodopi B.V, 186 pages, paperback ISBN 9042016140 £28.40
Thomas Paine, *Common Sense,* Penguin Books Great Ideas Series, 112 pages, paperback ISBN 0141018909 £4.99

Just about 20 years ago, with Jill Craigie at the top of her intellectual form, when she thought the cinema could raise all the arts to a higher degree of excellence, we got the news from a good source that at last a proper film was to be made on a subject which cried out for it: Thomas Paine.

He had been my number one revolutionary hero and, instructed perhaps by her love of revolutions, Rebecca West, he was high up on Jill's list too. It so happens that we had been together with several Indian friends who knew what we were seeing at the first-night showing of Richard Attenborough's *Ghandi* was the truly epic subject properly displayed. The actors contributed to the film's success but it was the vision of the great director testing his new instruments to the limit which would achieve the great results. Not so long after that night of triumph we were told that Attenborough was turning his imaginative mind to Thomas Paine as his next great subject. It could still happen, but meantime I must give readers an update on Thomas Paine matters. Some may recall that I have, on occasion, such is his important role in history, suggested changing the name of Trafalgar Square to Thomas Paine Square. It would be a nice compliment to the Americans and the French, since he played such an important part in achieving their freedom as well as ours.

However, I now report not the great film but three new books, which should remind us afresh how essential were the causes we honour today.

The first and the most significant is *These Are The Times: A Life of Thomas Paine* by Trevor Griffiths, who makes his dedication: 'For Richard Attenborough, comrade and conductor on this long march'. Such words might suggest that the march is ended, but not necessarily so. Here is the brilliant and truly original screenplay written by Griffiths for the film, and I hope that its publication may revive the idea of making it. Most of the scenes take place in America, but they speak again to the whole world. Griffiths is a true Painite, and I was sent this copy by an old friend who also qualifies for that title, Ken Coates, of the Bertrand Russell Peace Foundation in Nottingham.

The second book, Bernard Vincent's *The Transatlantic Republican: Thomas Paine and the Age of Revolutions*, offers a series of fresh lectures and reviews. Vincent has already played a leading role in restoring Paine's proper reputation in France. Paine himself never forgot his debt to the people of France and Paris in particular. But only with Vincent's scholarship and political insight has that association been properly restored. The other truly great contribution to this period was John Keane's book, *Tom Paine: A Political Life*, published by Bloomsbury on May 1, 1995. Never was there a better date to remind us of the even greater glory of July 14th which all those truly entitled to call themselves revolutionaries, the women even more than the men, must still celebrate. Keane then told the story better than ever before, and he would have been happy to acclaim those who are just catching up.

Third, Penguin has just published in its Great Ideas series, Thomas Paine's *Common Sense*, which first made him infamous. On December 3rd, the Thomas Paine Society held its annual meeting in London's Conway Hall, which is our regular meeting place. Without Conway Hall, without Moncure Conway, true revolutionaries of the modern age would have no such appropriate place to meet. Without his truly liberal ideas, embracing women as well as men, which he brought from America, we would still be living in the intellectual dark ages.

The more we look today on the persistent topicality of Paine's political ideas, the more we see for ourselves that it is the potency of his writing which prevails, and we may be all the more amazed to recall that Richard Carlile was imprisoned in 1823 for selling Paine's *Rights of Man*. Carlile concluded that matter thus: 'His pen continued an overmatch for the whole brood.'

Michael Foot

Where is Tom Paine?

Bruce Kuklick (Ed), *Thomas Paine*, Ashgate International Library of Essays in the History of Social and Political Thought, 514 pages, hardback ISBN 0 7546 2490 0 £125.00/$250
Paul Collins, *The Trouble with Tom*, Bloomsbury, 279 pages, hardback ISBN 0747577684 £12.99

Bruce Kuklick has assembled an extensive collection of essays on Thomas Paine, beginning with two significant overviews of the literature, which is clearly growing at a phenomenal speed. There are as many people who pray Tom Paine in aid as we can count, and the literature of his detractors, from Edmund Burke on down, would fill a sizeable library. The two bibliographical essays, by A. Owen Aldridge and Caroline Robbins, offer an adequate taster of this.

Aldridge points out that we still lack anything approaching a complete edition of Tom Paine's works, in spite of the fact that his writing resonates with sharp clarity. Paine used a number of pseudonyms, one of which echoes the Miltonic influence which helped to shape his outlook. Comus made his debut in the *Pennsylvania Packet* in March 1779, and brought its fire to bear on Governor Morris who was to become a perennial target.

Caroline Robbins begins with Paine's Quaker tradition: 'Everyone, he wrote, is finally his own teacher'. He seldom, she says, 'allowed five minutes to pass without seeking some improvement'.

Kuklick's book treats on six main subject areas: in addition to its survey of the literature, it includes a section on Paine's influence on the history of political thought, and another on Paine and the ideology of Republicanism. There is a fourth part on the social history of ideas, and a fifth on the literary quality of Paine's writings. The book concludes with two stirring treatments of Paine's influence on radical history, by Ian Dyck and Harvey J. Kaye. Kaye endorses the belief that the study of American radicals should be essential homework for this generation, because it will give heart to the victims of the erosion of democracy over the recent past.

Amen to that: but the really essential homework involves the story of where they failed, and why ...

Kuklick finishes his anthology with a reference to William Cobbett, who began by sharing an intense dislike, not to say phobia about the revolutionary Paine, but became a dedicated acolyte, going so far as to dig up Paine's bones in the United States and bring them to England, where he hoped they might receive a more reverent welcome, possibly interment in a mausoleum.

This story is taken up by Paul Collins, in *The Trouble with Tom*, which records 'the strange afterlife and times of Thomas Paine'. The story of the loss of Paine's bones is a complicated one, and it has given rise to a macabre book, which does not know the answer. But it finishes with a good question: *'Where is Tom Paine? Reader, where is he not?'*

James Jones

Secret Manipulation

Dianne Hayter, *Fightback! Labour's traditional right in the 1970s and 1980s,* **Manchester University Press, hardback ISBN 0719072700 £60.00, paperback ISBN 0719072719 £14.99**

This claims to be an insiders' account of how the right wing in the Labour Party regained the traditional pre-eminence it appeared to have lost following the fall of the Callaghan Government in 1979, thus preparing the way for its triumphant return in the form of New Labour.

In 1960 the left-right battle had swung towards the left with the adoption of a policy of unilateral nuclear disarmament at the Scarborough Conference – thanks to dedicated organisation by the Party's rank and file. This victory was ignored by the leadership – particularly in the Parliamentary Labour Party, who refused to acknowledge that the Party's official position had changed – and was subsequently reversed.

The rank and file took the position that there was little point in working to gain support for policies within the Party if, once carried, these were ignored by the leadership. They argued that the Party belonged to its members (which was certainly true at law) and not to a handful of Members of Parliament who had always assumed they had the right to appoint the Leader and determine the Party's policy. Although the Party was set up by trade unionists, they had always deferred to their parliamentary colleagues.

This approach led to the formation in the 1970s of the Campaign for Labour Party Democracy (CLPD), dedicated to securing constitutional changes that would make the Party more democratic, and more accountable to its members. It is generally accepted that it was CLPD's success in securing the mandatory re-selection of MPs by their constituencies before each general election that was the final straw that led to the breakaway of a right faction to form the SDP in 1981. They were so out of sympathy with their constituency parties and the National Executive that they were afraid they would not be re-adopted by their constituencies and therefore had nothing to lose by going it alone.

Hayter describes the limited efforts of the right in Parliament to organize against the left-controlled National Executive Committee, but she sees them as more concerned to safeguard their own jobs rather than to take up positions of principle which might leave them vulnerable to attack.

Much more effective, in Hayter's view, were the trade unionists in the secret St Ermine's Group whose aims were:

> 'taking control of the NEC and then to fashion the party outside the House into an election-winning entity. This would mean expelling Militant, changing head-office personnel and concentrating on winning back public support. Their first service to the party was not to defect in the aftermath of Wembly (1981); their second was to take control of the NEC by 1982: their third was to deliver the leadership to Kinnock, in whom they saw someone equally committed to the task of returning to government'.

By 1987, the right had gained control. Kinnock was leader and felt strong enough to start reshaping policy. With trade union backing he launched a Policy Review at the '87 Conference which, by '91, resulted in four reports which formed the basis of the 1992 manifesto. The Party dropped its opposition to the Common Market and returned to its traditional positions on defence and the mixed economy.

With the death of John Smith, in 1994, and the election of Tony Blair as leader, the ground was prepared for the further reforms of New Labour – restructuring the National Executive Committee to bring it under the control of Downing Street, together with the Party apparatus, with a so-called Chairman appointed by the Prime Minister. 'Spin' and 'control', the result of secret machinations of groups such as St Ermine's, became apparent for all to see, so that the Party became a laughing-stock to the general public and repugnant to its membership, which fell from 400,000 to less than 200,000 over the period of the Labour Government.

Opportunist to the end, the self-styled modernizers are now seeking to turn to their advantage the scandal of undeclared loans to the Labour Party in exchange for hoped-for peerages. They are arguing that such abuses would not occur if political parties were funded by the state. They would thus achieve their dream of doing away with members altogether; the political parties would thus become self-perpetuating oligarchies, answerable to no one but themselves.

At present we have an electoral system that has not produced majority rule since 1931 – the year of Labour's great débâcle. It could perhaps be defended on the grounds that single-member constituencies can, in theory, select their own Members of Parliament. There doesn't seem to be much other justification for a system which never manages to achieve democracy – that is, rule by the majority. With selection of MPs controlled by party officials with subventions from the state, ties with local constituencies will become meaningless, as with many of the continental party list systems, and our present electoral system will lose all legitimacy.

The trend towards secret manipulation, started by the St Ermine's Group, must be countered by moves towards openness and transparency at all levels in the Labour Party. The work of the Campaign for Labour Party Democracy is more important than ever.

Richard Fletcher

COMMUNICATION WORKERS UNION

May Day Greetings

Billy Hayes
General Secretary

Pat O'Hara
President